Reiki Journeys
Personal Stories of Healing, Strength, and
Renewal
Eve Smyth

Sanctum With Eve

Eve Smyth, LLC

Published by Eve Smyth, LLC

1886 N. Decatur Rd

Decatur, Georgia 30030

Smith, Eve

ISBN: 979-8-9919094-0-2

eBook: 979-8-9919094-1-9

Cover design by: Isabel Romano

Copyediting by: Kate Crofts

Interior design by: Eve Smith

Sanctum With Eve
www.sanctumwithevesmyth.com

Disclaimer

The content of this book is intended for entertainment and educational purposes only. It is not meant to be a substitute for professional medical care, diagnosis, or advice from a qualified healthcare practitioner. The experiences, stories and practices shared here reflect personal journeys and are not intended to replace any medical treatment or therapeutic interventions. Always seek the guidance of a licensed medical professional for any health concerns or conditions. The authors and contributors assume no responsibility or liability for any actions taken by readers based on the information provided in this book.

Acknowledgments

I offer immense gratitude to my students without whom this book would not be possible. Their stories were an inspiration to sharing my own story. Thank you for the continual suggestions that this book be written, coaching, and support. It was in community that this book was written.

A special thanks to: Chandra Maharaj, Shaneka Hunter, Anthony Jones, Susanne McMurry, and Felicia Holden for your support and contribution.

My family and Kathryn Crofts talked me through multiple rewrites. My superwoman mom, Alice Smith, never turned down a last minute "can you read this one more time?" request.

Thank you to Claudia Ellet who read the work and offered suggestions.

Deep gratitude to my teachers: Stephen Clasper, Pervin Clasper, Mark Nelson, Tenzin Lama, Don Conreaux, Dr. Mitch Nur, Aiden McIntyre, Tim Byford, Hersha, Institute of Applied Holistic Health Sciences in Thailand, the monks in Xiahe, Emei Shan, Chiang Mai, and the many other places I was blessed to experience. Without these experiences, this book could not be written. Thank you all for sharing your time, attention, and knowledge.

There is an immense body of work from film to the written word that has supported my development and understanding over the years.

You will find the list under References & Further Reading. To all those authors, editors, directors, and everyone who made possible the birth of the work, I thank you.

I am certain that I have missed a few people. If I have, please know that it was not intentional.

Finally, thank you for buying this book! Because of your purchase, others will benefit. All the profit after expenses goes to charity.

Contents

Chapter 1

New Beginnings

This work has taken a lifetime of study to create. For years, I chased the rush of last-minute deadlines, my own adrenaline becoming fuel. Procrastination pushed me to stay up, caffeinated and burning through projects, using stress to power through. The extreme rush of energy was me using my nervous system and brain to create and maintain a high. Over time, this habit drained my health and joy.

Everything shifted when I found myself in Asia with the Peace Corps and other organizations. There, I learned different ways of existing. In China, midday rest was customary and a stark contrast to my ingrained "push through" mentality. At first, I resisted; there was always more to experience, more to do. However, when everything, including many restaurants, shut down during the midday break there was nothing that could be done. Even the uncle and auntie (terms of respect) who religiously guarded the front of the university housing where I stayed were nowhere to be seen.

It took a good six months of watching people milling about outside for their after-lunch stroll to improve digestion that I began to wonder why I was not one of them. What was it that kept me so tied to the idea of "getting things done?"

I lay down to nap and all the things that I was not doing played like a movie in my mind. Getting up, I wrote a list of all the things that came up and laid back down. More things to do arose in my mind.

Every day that I attempted to rest, this struggle arose and I saw that my body and mind had been trained to run nonstop.

The Chinese approach emphasized lifelong care, a concept foreign to me. Trained from a young age, the daily exercise blared over the speakers at schools as early as 6 a.m. Everyone of my university students took part in the exercises as 1, 2, 3, ...8 in Mandarin echoed across the campus.

Many of the same exercises they did were repeated by adults in parks across the city. These exercises assisted people by moving energy around their bodies, stretching their tendons, their muscles, and keeping them limber over the years. They understood the lifelong benefit of continual stretching and movement over time would benefit them in 50 or 60 years.

I was in my twenties and healthy; thinking of myself in my forties or eighties was too abstract. Yet, surrounded by such wisdom, I began a journey of unlearning nonstop work and rushing around while learning balance and harmony. My journey continues to this day.

One unforgettable moment came at a Shaolin kung fu performance at Mount Emei (□□□) in Sichuan. Time stood still. The mountain was draped in mist, hiding its ornate temples, but I did not need eyes to see the beauty. Awe, like a purring cat, crept into my heart. The Shaolin performers dazzled with sword performance to music. With actions that betrayed thousands of hours of practice and a defiance of gravity, I watched spellbound when they were not impaled as they balanced their bodies on the blade of a sword or flew ten feet across the stage in a leap.

After the performance as we were greeted by the quiet hum of nature and Buddhist temple life, a deep stillness settled inside me, relaxing my body in a way that I had never felt before.

It was the beginning. Searching for this elusive sacred stillness created the story of my life until finding it through Reiki.

Traveling across China, I felt this stillness again in the power of Tibetan throat singing and temple instruments in Xiahe. As I rested against the temple wall and the sound washed through me, my body began to release its hold on the constant drive for productivity, drawn instead to a sacred state of peace. An inner place that is accessible to me through a life infused with sound, meditation, and prayer.

In another chapter of my life, that experience might have sparked a profound awakening, shifting my entire being. But it did not. Within a month, I fell back into familiar patterns of productivity, though my stress levels, while still present, were not as intense. The peaceful, calming effect of the throat singing, fresh mountain air, and wide-open landscapes in Xiehe stayed with me, accessible now through my meditation practice. In those twenty minutes, even a moment or two of stillness was enough to reconnect me with that sense of peace.

I continued learning from monk talks in Chiang Mai (Thailand), Tibetan yoga in Elista (Russia), and yoga teacher training in Hong Kong (China). At that time, in the countries where I lived there was not yet a plethora of English books, movies, shows, and apps on energy to rely on. With every return to the states, I bought books on these topics, read them and then I shipped out again overseas. I sought knowledge in English in Asia and the other countries I have lived in whenever I could, gradually finding familiar threads in the common fables and morality stories they shared to drive home a specific idea. As each teacher shared their unique take on the stories, it was how they personalized their stories with tales from their lives which resonated. To honor this tradition, I retell some of the concepts through my stories and with my own twist. I have also invited my students to share how Reiki has changed their life.

To all these experiences and teachers I extend my eternal gratitude. They offered me their shoulders to stand on when I was unable to make my own way. Thank you. I now offer my shoulders to others.

Chapter 2

Introduction: A Journey Into Reiki

Eve Smyth

Welcome to a journey of transformation, healing, and empowerment. This book presents Reiki, a gentle yet profound healing practice originating in Japan over 100 years ago. Reiki is a holistic method that can bring about balance in both the body and mind. We are often taught to rely solely on medicine to restore harmony when we are unwell. While medicine plays a crucial role, we sometimes find that physical ailments persist because the underlying causes—stress, emotional imbalances, or pain patterns within the body—remain unaddressed. Reiki invites you to look beyond the physical, addressing the emotional, mental, and energetic layers of our being.

While often misunderstood, Reiki is not associated with any religion or organization. This book was born out of the desire to demystify Reiki and show its incredible range and effectiveness. Reiki is not a one-size-fits-all method. It is tailored to the needs of the individual, always working in alignment with your specific gifts and what is for your highest good.

This book is a collection of stories from a diverse group of Reiki practitioners, all of whom have studied Reiki with me. Each is on their own life journey with unique challenges. What unites them is a shared desire for balance, harmony, and healing, not only in their own lives but also in the lives of those they touch.

The stories you will read here illustrate just how varied and powerful Reiki can be, from helping someone recover from panic attacks to guiding another to overcome their fear of public speaking, to providing relief from chronic migraines.

As a Reiki practitioner for over a decade, my purpose in teaching Reiki has always been to empower others to create a richly balanced life for themselves. As I worked with clients over the years I noticed that many would book a session to understand what was happening in their body. It can be frustrating when you do everything "right" and the body is not in balance. This leaves you stressed, in pain, and ready for change.

Reiki teaches us that no person's body or life experience is exactly the same. The body will communicate its needs to us if we slow down and listen. As a Reiki teacher, I hope to empower you to listen to your body, mind, and spirit; to come into balance; and to call forth healing. Each one of us has this potential. Reiki will help you harmonize your body.

Not reserved for the few or the spiritually elite, Reiki is open to everyone. Whether you are someone seeking relief from physical pain, emotional turmoil, or simply looking to grow spiritually, Reiki has a way of meeting you where you are and giving you what you need.

The stories shared in this book are gifts. They are windows into the lives of people just like you—people who were curious, unsure, and sometimes even skeptical at first about Reiki. They learned Reiki, embraced the practice, and experienced profound changes that extended far beyond what they imagined as Reiki practice coupled with curiosity allows a person to expand.

It is important to note that not every outcome in these pages may reflect your own experience, Reiki will always work in a way that is uniquely suited to you. Healing, in its many forms, is deeply personal, and Reiki meets each person in the place where they need it most.

I invite you to read these stories with an open heart and mind. Let the experiences of these practitioners inspire you, and remember that Reiki is not just for others—it is for you too, whenever you feel ready to explore it.

With love and light,

Eve Smyth

Chapter 3

Reiki: A Path to Balance and Well-being

In today's world of overwhelm, finding work-life balance and harmony can feel like an elusive goal. Many people are searching for ways to reconnect with their bodies, minds, and spirits—seeking a method to release stress, heal from past experiences, or simply enhance their overall well-being. One powerful, yet gentle practice helping millions of people around the world work towards and achieve balance is Reiki.

Reiki is one type of energetic modality such as yoga, sound therapy, meditation, etc. These modalities may use a combination of meditation, breathwork, and movement to align the energy of the body, mind, and spirit. A Japanese healing technique, Reiki, taps into the universal life energy that flows through all living things. It is non-invasive, deeply relaxing, and a powerful tool for self-healing. Reiki can be used for many things from pain relief to spiritual growth. If you have never heard of Reiki before, that is okay. Like the gentle flow of Reiki, this introduction will help you learn what Reiki is, how it works, and why it might be the key to unlocking more peace and vitality in your life. Then, you will learn from real practitioners who offer you stories of deep personal and physical healing of back pain and fear of public speaking, as well as how Reiki has helped open them up to working with others.

What Is Reiki?

At its core, Reiki is a simple yet profound healing technique that originated in Japan in the early twentieth century. The system was developed by Dr. Mikao Usui, a Japanese Buddhist monk. In the book, *The Spirit of Reiki* (2001), William Rand writes that Reiki was the manifestation of Mikao Usui's childhood desire. In Dr. Usui's early years, he studied Qi Gong at the Tendai Buddhist temple. Qi Gong combines breath, movement, and meditation to assist the flow of "qi" (life force energy) through the body. Reiki scholar Rand continues: Dr. Usui was frustrated because the Qi Gong healing technique is exhausting. You have to gather the energy in your body, give the healing, and then recover. Usui knew that there had to be a way to offer profound healings without depleting personal stores of energy. Dr. Usui devoted his life to learning what he could about healing practices and medicine.

In his 50s, Dr. Usui had become a Buddhist monk and decided to pursue healing. He trained rigorously and prepared himself for a retreat where his intention was to find a way to heal others that would not tire the practitioner out. With this *intention*, Dr. Usui meditated for twenty-one days at Mount Kurma, near the Tendai Buddhist temple. On the twenty-first day, Dr. Usui received knowledge to access and channel healing energy that could bring the body, mind, and spirit back into balance. The experience at the mountain was his attunement to the Reiki energy.

To receive a healing technology while meditating on a mountain seems like an incredible tale.

How is it possible that one man can receive this kind of knowing or understanding?

The human mind is vast and we only understand a small portion of it. Partly because we do not know where exactly *it* resides. We also do not completely understand what *it* is.

- Is the mind emotions?

- Is *it* thoughts and emotions?

- What exactly makes up the mind?

In 1985, Dr. Valerie V. Hunt wrote about her work as a scientist studying human consciousness. In her book *Infinite Mind* (1995), she explores how scientists like Einstein, Newton, and others discovered great wisdom by meditating and entering different states of consciousness—similar to what Dr. Usui did on the mountain when he received the knowledge of Reiki.

Dr. Hunt found through her research that everything in the world, including humans, has an energy field. This energy field is real and can be measured using scientific tools as it flows in and around our bodies. Energy is measured in terms of frequency and vibration, and by looking at these measurements, you can get an idea of the health of an organism—including a human.

Dr. Hunt's research also showed that our minds and energy fields are connected. She called this connection the "mind-field." The mind-field is influenced by our thoughts and emotions, and it *can also be affected by the thoughts and emotions of other people.* More recently, Drs. Candance Pert (1997) and Shamani Jain (2021), among others, have shown through western science how our thoughts and emotions impact the immune system. For example, when you are emotionally charged with grief, stress, or something else, your immune system is impacted and it may be easier for you to get sick.

Before looking at the immune system in more detail, the effect that your connection with others has on how you think and feel is important to note. An example might be when you listen to music. Have you noticed that your mood can change depending on the emotions in the song? You might feel happy, sad, or even angry just from the music. Your vibration is entraining to the music which means it is automatically shifting to match the frequencies. As this entrainment or shift occurs, you will experience the emotion of the song. After the song finishes, you may continue to hold onto the emotion it evoked, or you might choose to focus on a new emotion.

To illustrate further within a balancing context, think about how you feel when you talk to a friend who is upset. You might listen and offer advice and care. At the end of the conversation, you might have helped the person feel better. Part of the reason for this is that your energy field was vibrating differently than your friend. Because of this, as you spoke their energy field changed until its vibrations were closer in alignment to yours. The energy field changes then impacted the mind and body, providing emotional relief for them. While Dr. Hunt measured this process in her work, Barbara Ann Brennan describes purposefully using the energy field around the clients in the book *Hands Of Light* (1988). More references on this topic are listed in the reference section at the end of the book.

The mind-field also explains why we sometimes know things we cannot easily explain. Have you ever thought about someone, and then they called you? Or had a sense of what someone was going to say or do something before they did? These experiences are connected to how our mind-fields interact. And, it is a part of what Dr. Hunt called "the human vibrations of consciousness." In *Hands of Light*, Brennan shares activities and practices to develop these forms of consciousness. The *Yoga Sutras of Patanjali*, thought to be written around the first century, provide theory and practice on developing the ability to consciously access these types of psychic phenomena which is inherent to all through the practice of yoga.

Consciousness is the state of being aware of and able to think about yourself, your surroundings, and *your thoughts*. This can also sometimes be called awareness or mindfulness. Consciousness is what allows us to experience and respond to the world around us, to reflect on our own existence, and to make decisions.

In other words, consciousness is your awareness of being alive, your thoughts, emotions, and the world you are in. When you are awake and alert, you are conscious; when you are asleep or unconscious (in a coma, for example), it is often believed that your awareness is either greatly reduced or gone. However, Dr. Hunt found this to be untrue. Our consciousness is always plugged in and listening. In her research she found that people who were labeled unconscious during a surgery or considered comatose could recall exactly what was said and done when under a certain type of hypnosis. Anita Moorjani, who had a near death experience in 2006, reported in her book, *Dying to Be Me* (2012), that she was able to describe, with accuracy and in detail, what the doctors and nurses who were assisting her body were doing and saying throughout the time she was in a coma. Even with multiple pieces of evidence to the contrary, many believe that if you are not awake, your consciousness is asleep too.

Thus, consciousness is a complex and widely debated topic in fields like philosophy, psychology, and neuroscience. It includes things like:

1. Awareness: Being aware of yourself, your thoughts, emotions, and surroundings.

2. Thoughts: Your ability to think, reason, and reflect on your experiences.

3. Perception: How you see, hear, and feel things happening around you.

4. Intentionality: Your ability to focus your mind on something, like when you are thinking about a problem or making a plan.

5. Sense of self: Your awareness of yourself as an individual, separate from others.

However, there is a higher level of consciousness. This Consciousness is experienced as a state of oneness that is eternal, compassionate, and all-knowing (Jain, 2021). Consciousness of this magnitude is what is often meant when speaking of the divine which is why Consciousness is written with a capital "C" (Jain, 2021). Of course, we still do not fully understand how Consciousness works and where it comes from in our body and mind. It continues to be a mystery that we seek to unravel.

How does Consciousness relate to Dr. Usui and Reiki?

By going into deep meditation and connecting with Consciousness, Dr. Usui was able to channel the knowledge of Reiki. He tapped into higher wisdom from the universe. Later descriptions the day he received the knowledge of Reiki, it is reported that a radiant light streamed into the top of his head carrying all the symbols. Like receiving a download.

This is similar to how Einstein worked. He had a practice of going into a type of deep meditation, altering the brainwave state of his mind (Zajonic, 2011). In this state, many of the questions he held were answered. With practice, accessing your mind-field and Consciousness can lead to amazing discoveries, just as it did for Dr. Usui and many other great thinkers through meditation and sound.

Reiki Defined

Now that we see how it is possible to channel a healing technology like Reiki, let us explore what Reiki is in more detail. The word "Reiki" itself is derived from two Japanese words: Rei, meaning "universal" or "spiritual wisdom/power," and Ki, meaning "life energy." Together, Reiki can be understood as "spiritually guided life energy" or "universal life energy."

This universal life energy flows through each of us, keeping us physically and mentally healthy. It is called different names around the world. Some of those names include: qi, chi, ki, or prana. When our life energy is disrupted—by stress, accidental or environmental trauma, repetitive injury, negative thought patterns, high levels of pollution, or even just the daily grind—our bodies and minds become unbalanced, which may lead to illness, emotional turbulence, or general fatigue. Reiki rebalances.

This life energy is said to flow through all living things and can become blocked or imbalanced due to stress, environmental factors, accidents, illness, or emotional struggles. Practitioners are trained to channel Reiki energy through their body and into the hands. First, practitioners work on themselves by placing their hands over or above a location in their body to clear energy blockages and promote natural healing. In other words, Reiki removes any obstacles to healing while activating your inner healing capabilities. Then, once a practitioner has worked through their imbalances, they must realign their lifestyle to avoid de-harmonizing their body and mind.

Reiki can be practiced in various forms. You may have seen all types of Reiki advertised from fire healing Reiki to Shamanic Reiki to something else. These are not Reiki as Usui taught it. What we know of the traditional Usui Reiki system in the west is adapted from the work of Dr. Usui by Hawayo Takata. A woman of Japanese origin, upon becoming ill in the 1930s, she went to Japan for treatment. At one of Usui's Reiki clinics, she became well and wanted to learn the healing system. One of Dr. Usui's students, Dr. Hayashi, initiated her to the highest rank. He continued to train and work with her. When they returned to the US, Hayashi and Takata taught lectures, gave treatments, and taught Reiki (Lübeck, Petter, & Rand, 2001). Many of her students, and their students have created Reiki training manuals based on the methodology Takata employed. Several are listed under further resources in the back.

Most Reiki systems of learning in the west are the Takata method. During World War II and for a little while beyond, Reiki practitioners in Japan who directly studied with Dr. Usui and his students did not promote themselves beyond Japan. Therefore, it is likely that the teachers near you studied a lineage based on the Takata method. My lineage is Takata.

Dr. Mikao Usui
Dr. C. Hayashi
Mrs. Hawayo Takata
Phyllis Lei Furumoto
Dr. Adolfo
Mrs. Rashmi Solanki
Ravi Hooja
Pervin S. Clasper
Stephen Clasper
Eve Smith (Smyth)

Because Takata changed the way she taught Reiki from the traditional method does *not* mean there is an impact in a practitioner's ability to give Reiki. Here's why: Reiki, coming from the divine, is an intelligent energy. Not only does it channel through a practitioner bringing balance and harmony to that person, but it also streams differently for different people. If you have a regular dedicated practice, Reiki will begin to teach you how to use it in wonderful and unexpected ways.

Take me for example, as I was working with Reiki it began teaching me to align the energetic pathways of the body. When I described what I was doing to a practitioner of another type of energy work, she said Reiki had taught me the healing technology she worked with. I was shocked. Not only was Reiki assisting my clients getting balanced, it taught me a different type of healing technology.

Cycling back to my earlier statement: *"You may have seen all types of Reiki advertised from fire healing Reiki to Shamanic Reiki to something else."* What my experience shows is that when someone comes up with a "new" type of Reiki, this is really a new type of Reiki that was channeled to them because of their unique talents and gifts. Just because it is not taught in the traditional style does not mean that it is "wrong" or "ineffective." Just because the practitioner teaching it has incredible stories, does not mean that your experience with Reiki will be the same. What you want to look for in a teacher is a deep understanding of core Reiki practices and principles, continual professional development, and that they have a consistent, if not daily, self-Reiki practice.

Reiki is the ultimate teacher, a truth that Dr. Usui told his students.

The Takata method of Reiki which adapted the traditional methodology to three levels of learning is as follows:

Reiki Level 1: Introduction to the practice and learning how to channel Reiki energy primarily for self-healing. At this level you complete 21-days of self-healing before you work on anyone else. It is important to balance yourself first. The reason for this is that you will never be truly effective or in balance if you are not actively working towards healing yourself. If you are not in balance when your bio-field interacts with your client, you will not have enough of an electric charge to assist in bringing (entraining) others into balance. A bio-field is a field of energy around the body that is a combination of information and bioelectromagnetic energy created from organ and cellular functions. This encompasses what is known as the subtle energy fields (Jain, 2021). It is measurable and changeable. If you are out of balance, the bio-field may not be as strong as someone who is in balance. Due to this, Reiki may work on you first rather than channeling through you to the client.

Please note that even if this happens, the person a Reiki practitioner is working on will have no negative impact. Reiki will simply heal the Reiki practitioner first. Whatever Reiki energy is left over will move through to the client so they will still receive some benefit.

After you have practiced on yourself for a time, then, you might practice with close friends or family. At this level you will likely begin to experience synchronicities. Synchronicities are occurrences of events that seem or appear meaningfully related but have no obvious connection. For example, you read a post then have a conversation later that day where the other person brings up the same content of the post and feel like you are receiving a message. What I have experienced through Reiki is that the synchronicities in my life are far more complex and dynamic than the basic definition of synchronicity implies.

Reiki Level 2: Expands the practitioner's ability to channel energy over distance and with more intensity. In Reiki Level 2 you will also complete 21-days of self-practice. You can think of Level 2 as an up-leveling. Where Level 1 is like surfing a small wave in Florida, Level 2 is surfing a mega wave in Hawaii. The 21-days of self-practice are needed to adjust to the new wave. Many practitioners report at this stage they experience profound rebalancing of the body and shifts such as psychic development, in addition to landing their dream house, desired job, or meaningful relationship.

Reiki Level 3 (Master): Deepens one's spiritual connection by again working on healing yourself. Becoming a Reiki master does not mean that you have mastery of Reiki. This is a misunderstanding. What it means is that you have come to an agreement inside yourself that you will spend the rest of your life *working towards* mastery.

Mastery level means that your full self will be exposed to you over time and with love so that you can see who you really are and whether it is in alignment with how you are acting and reacting in the world. A Reiki master must work through who they think they are and who they actually are so that they can see and embody who they would like to be.

It is very common with diligent practice to find yourself feeling deep a connection to the universe, the world around you, your intuition, and your psychic gifts. You will find yourself less reactive, feeling more in control (regardless of the state of the world around you), happier, and more joyful. This is often what naturally occurs with continual practice.

How Does Reiki Work?

A Reiki session typically lasts anywhere from forty-five to ninety minutes. It may be completed sitting up or lying down. It is common for those receiving Reiki to lie fully clothed on a massage table. During the session, the practitioner places their hands gently on or just above the body, allowing Reiki energy to flow from the universe through the crown or top of their head, into their heart and out through their hands to the recipient. This is a channeled energy, it comes from the universal life source rather than a human source. Thus Dr. Usui received the knowledge he was searching for: A healing art that will not drain the energy of the practitioner.

The recipient may feel warmth, tingling, or a deep sense of calm and relaxation as the energy begins to activate their inner healer to remove blockages and promote balance in the body.

It is important to note that **Reiki is not a replacement for medical treatment**, but rather a complementary therapy. Reiki works well alongside other forms of healthcare and you will find it in prominent hospitals around the world. Some of the ways it is used is to relax patients before surgery, manage pain after surgery and during chemotherapy, among others.

Short and Sweet Summary

Usui Reiki is a Japanese healing technique that channels universal life energy to promote balance, healing, and relaxation in the body, mind, and spirit. Developed by Dr. Mikao Usui in the early twentieth century, it is widely used today.

Natural healing and balance is promoted by channeling Reiki through the practitioner's hands. Reiki is a non-invasive, gentle practice used to help alleviate stress, pain, and emotional struggles.

There are three levels of Reiki learning:

1. Reiki Level 1 focuses on self-healing.

2. Reiki Level 2 expands the ability to heal others, including from a distance.

3. Reiki Level 3 deepens spiritual connection and lifelong commitment to Reiki.

Reiki is a channeled complementary therapy, often used alongside medical treatments to support emotional well-being, manage pain, and promote healing.

Key Points:

1. Energy Field and Consciousness:

- Dr. Valerie Hunt's research shows everything, including humans, has an energy field that can be measured by frequency and vibration.

- Dr. Shamini Jain shows that a Reiki or other energy practitioner uses the bio-field to connect the healing energy with their client.

- Our thoughts and emotions, as well as the emotions of others, affect our energy field, a concept Hunt termed the "mind-field."

- Consciousness and energy fields are interconnected and influence each other.

2. The Reiki Healing Process:

- Reiki can be given anywhere, including distance, and at any time, though it is most common for the receiver to be lying on a massage table.

- Reiki clears energy blockages and activates the body's natural healing abilities.

- It is practiced by channeling energy through the practitioner's hands.

- Reiki works on both physical and emotional levels, relieving stress and promoting well-being.

- A Reiki session can be as short as a minute, but is often given for forty-five minutes to an hour.

3. Reiki Basics:

- Reiki is a Japanese healing technique developed by Dr. Mikao Usui.

- It taps into the universal life energy to restore balance and healing in the body, mind, and spirit.

- Reiki is non-invasive and deeply relaxing, promoting self-healing, and spiritual growth.

- A qualified practitioner is the only one who can pass the ability to do Reiki through what is called an "Attunement" according to Dr. Mikao Usui.

- Anyone can learn and use Reiki.

- Reiki is intelligent and will go where needed.

- Reiki may continue to teach a practitioner innovative ways to use it.

- Reiki cannot be manipulated.

4. Complementary Nature of Reiki:
- Reiki is not a substitute for medical treatment but complements it by promoting relaxation, managing pain, and aiding recovery.

- It is used in hospitals worldwide for stress relief before surgery, pain management, and during chemotherapy.

- Reiki is not a religion, philosophy, or organization.

Chapter 4

Is Reiki A Scam?

How an Academic Became a Believer.

The heat in New Delhi was stifling, so I stayed indoors to avoid roasting. A flier near the guest house's breakfast table advertised Reiki as an add-on option to our homestay. *Why not try this Reiki thing*, I thought. The flier stated that Reiki had profound results in healing. Sleep did not come easily to me and the vitals on my health check were off balance. I asked the owner if there was an availability. She nodded and led me up a narrow staircase to the top floor, where I lay on a comfortable lounger.

"I will be holding my hands above your body. You may or may not feel the energy." The owner sat across from me, watching to ensure I closed my eyes.

"Close your eyes and set an intention for this healing," she instructed as she turned on the window box air conditioning for that room and placed a small blanket over me. There was a flick of a match then the smell of sandalwood drifted in and out as the hum of the ac unit relaxed me.

Forty-five minutes later, I woke up to find her sitting in the exact same position across from me, looking expectant.

"What did you feel?" she asked. I slept the entire time. Disappointment washed over me.

"Nothing," I said, "I felt nothing." I pulled my lips into a smile to soften the frustration in my voice.

Sensing my irritation, she said, "Don't worry, this happens to many people. You won't always feel something during Reiki, but trust that it is working."

I still wasn't sure she'd sat in the chair across from me reading a novel while I took a nap. But I tried to resist the thought as it worked its way into my consciousness: Was this a scam? I buried the thought but it kept trying to surface. A person comes in, feels nothing, then you say, don't worry it really worked. I asked, "How do we know it works if I don't feel anything," before I could stop myself.

"Reiki is universal healing energy," she explained. "We're all connected to it."

That wasn't an answer and I was like a tic on a hound—hungry for more information. "But wouldn't that mean it's already healing me? That I wouldn't need someone else to direct it?"

"Sometimes your body gets out of balance, and Reiki helps restore it," she said. Getting out of balance felt true. It was why I'd booked an appointment to begin with—my body is off.

"So, what's the science behind it? How does it actually work?" I asked, pressing for something concrete to sink my teeth into.

"Some things we just have to have faith in," she replied.

The smile that pulled the corners of my mouth didn't make it to my eyes. I nodded, hiding my skepticism. Faith was one thing, but I trusted science. Why couldn't she explain how this worked? Even the most basic explanation would suffice. "Trust me, it worked" wasn't enough. I paid her $200 and went back to my room, unimpressed. Reiki and I had broken up before we even got together.

Or so I thought.

Life had other plans for me.

A few years later, I was in Bali, taking a break from my university work in Afghanistan. At the guest house, I met an older Australian man. One evening, as the sun set, we sat on the balcony, watching the light change over the rice fields. His joy for life was palpable. He delighted in the colors and the balmy breeze that chased away the mosquitos.

I wanted that joy. The weight of anxiety had begun to smother mine, so I asked him, "What's your secret to enjoying life with such wonder?"

"Reiki," he said, eyes twinkling as he looked at the sky, missing my eye roll. *Reiki? You've got to be kidding me*, I thought.

"What about Reiki makes you say that?" I asked, my skepticism obvious. But he didn't seem to care.

"I was supposed to be dead," he said matter-of-factly, "I've been in full kidney failure for the past seven years." According to science, he told me, he shouldn't have survived seven years of failing kidneys. Through radical changes in his diet by cutting out all sugar and spice and regular visits to a Balinese Reiki master, his health had dramatically improved.

"Western medicine only took me so far," he signed in contentment. "I had to expand the menu to heal."

I blinked in disbelief. Before I could stop myself, the next words out of my mouth were, "Can you help me book an appointment?" How could Reiki be so profound for him when my experience in India had been a nap? *Had my disbelief clouded my thinking?*

He smiled, lifted his phone, and scheduled a session for me the next day.

The following afternoon, we arrived at a collection of huts, which served as a guest house for backpackers. The Australian pointed out the Reiki hut and disappeared for his session. I struck up conversations with a few backpackers lounging around, just to make sure the place was legitimate. Then, I wandered through the nearby streets, waiting for my turn.

When the Australian emerged from his session, he looked refreshed. Bowing to the Reiki master, his arm swept towards the door indicating for me to enter.

"Enjoy your time," the Aussie said as the Reiki master waved him off and gestured for me to enter the hut. After leaving my shoes outside, I stepped into a cool, comfortable room with a large massage table. He motioned for me to lie down and adjusted the pillow under my head.

Determined not to fall asleep this time, I clutched a small stone, dangling my hand off the side of the table. If I nodded off, the stone would slip out of my grasp. The sound of it hitting the floor would wake me. Turns out, I didn't need to be that clever.

The Reiki master stood behind me, vigorously rubbing his hands together. My muscles tensed as I felt him aim his palms at me. Suddenly, fire seemed to explode in my head and shoot down the right side of my body. He quickly pulled his hands away, shaking them as if he too had felt the heat. Muttering something in Balinese, he said, "You think too much. You need to stop thinking."

Truth.

He approached my head like someone nearing a coiled snake, testing the air with one hand around my temples before applying the other. This time, his hands never touched me, but the energy flowed like a gentle waterfall over and around my head. The rest of the session was filled with this soft, gentle energy, bringing a sense of balance and calm to my body and mind.

I was *WRONG*. Reiki is real—and wonderful. That night I slept like a log. Over the next 2 weeks I felt no constant undertow of stress.

My trip to Bali confirmed that Reiki can offer deep comfort and help the body regain balance. Reiki also offers good sleep and release of stress.

During my next annual health check in Bangkok, I took Level 1 Reiki. This class showed me what I hadn't known during my first Reiki experience in India, and what the woman there did not explain: Reiki often relaxes you by activating your parasympathetic nervous system. When you enter this "rest and digest" state, it is common to fall asleep because your inner healer has been activated. Your inner healer is your body's innate intelligence that knows what the body needs to come into balance and how to activate that healing capacity. This is a sign that the body is doing its internal work. While the woman in India had not explained it in a way that made sense to me, Reiki had worked; she had put me to sleep within *seconds*.

And maybe that first encounter helped me get to a place where the next time I received Reiki, I experienced it as I did.

Key Points Summary:

- Reiki activates the parasympathetic nervous system which is responsible for repairing the body.

- When combined with lifestyle changes, Reiki can have a profound healing effect.

- Reiki reduces stress.

- After a Reiki session, sleep can be restored for a few days.

- Every Reiki experience is different.

- Falling asleep during a Reiki session is one of many signs the Reiki is working!

Chapter 5
The Essence of the Reiki Mindset

The Five Principles

Reiki begins with five simple yet powerful principles that Dr. Mikao Usui, the founder of Reiki, believed were essential. People often get stuck in certain emotions or thought patterns. What we think and say to ourselves deeply affects our well-being.

Research shows that when you focus on love and gratitude, it does not just affect your mind—it affects your body, too. Loving compassion and gratitude make it easier for Reiki, which is often described as a loving hug, to pass through you and help you heal. It is believed that Dr. Usui created the Five Principles of Reiki to help practitioners maintain a peaceful, focused state with this in mind. A state of loving compassion and gratitude allow the channeled energy to flow more freely, making the healing more effective. These five principles assist in shaping your mindset, which shapes how you feel and respond to the world around you.

Here are the Five Principles of Reiki:
- Just for today, I will live the attitude of gratitude.

- Just for today, I will not worry.

- Just for today, I will not anger.

- Just for today, I will do my work honestly.

- Just for today, I will honor others.

Each of these principles is designed to keep you grounded in the present moment, where healing happens best. They remind you to focus on emotions like gratitude and kindness, which are key to harmonizing yourself and those you help.

The next few sections will explore each principle in detail to show how they may change your life.

Chapter 6
Living in Gratitude

Gratitude Shifts Your Focus

To live in gratitude means to be fully present and aware of the abundance that constantly surrounds you in each moment. It is about recognizing the beauty in what you have, instead of focusing on what you do not have. When you are focused on gratitude for what you have, you feel good. You may notice that in feeling gratitude for your life and everything in it, more people and opportunities you can be excited about come your way.

Social media often strips away gratitude, leaving comparison and judgment in its wake. Have you felt lacking in some way: Experiences, relationships, material items, or appearances? When you feel like you do not measure up, you start believing that you are not enough.

This mindset of lack feeds itself. Once you start believing you are not enough, your thoughts can spiral into more self-criticism and judgment. You begin to convince yourself that you do not deserve certain things—whether it is success, happiness, or even basic well-being. These negative thoughts shape how you live your life, influencing the choices you make and the opportunities you allow yourself to pursue.

For example, if I constantly feel that I am not good enough, I might begin to believe that I do not deserve the life I want—whether that is a certain home, a fulfilling career, or even a vacation. I might say to myself, "I make an abundance of money," or "I *deserve* to be happy," but deep down I may not actually believe those words. My unconscious mind, which has absorbed the belief that I do not *deserve* these things, will continue to shape my life. As a result, I might struggle to make ends meet or never take that vacation, even though I say I *want* those things.

This often-repeated principle comes from Hermetics, who is credited with saying, if you focus on the state of wanting you will always be wanting.

I do not believe that the word **deserve** has potential to be life changing. Often I hear the term *deserve* used as a source of permission for something you do not believe you should have (a cupcake, gym time, buying an item or product).

Deserve can also be used to talk yourself into the righteousness of something that is not entirely correct. There can be a disconnect between what the mind wants and what is in our best interest when we use the word *deserve*.

We know that eating refined sugar and carbohydrates are not ideal for the body. You might have completed an incredible project today at work that was the culmination of many weeks of hard work and frequent stress over deadlines. You are thinking about treating yourself to a couple of chocolate frosted cupcakes after work – after all, you earned it. This desire, or thought, stems from the mind and is likely correlated to a habit or behavior that developed over time. The habit is hard work = favorite treat. That becomes, I *deserve* a chocolate frosted cupcake for completing this incredible project. Then, that becomes *I want* or, *I need* a chocolate frosted cupcake. Have you ever noticed that as soon as you believe you deserve something your mind will not let you forget that thing? You may even go out of your way to get it.

This is hard! There is no shame or judgment in the desire for a cupcake, donut, or whatever. Nor am I trying to add any. Rather, I am trying to show how once the mind becomes fixed on getting an outcome, it is very hard to resist or distract it without beginning to feel upset. And, the mind will fix on anything, even if it is not "good" for you because the mind does not always use discernment.

Cycling back to the cupcake. Most of the time we give ourselves little treats throughout the day or as a reward for outstanding work. Do you stop to look at whether or not the treats that you are giving yourself are in your best interest? Here I am not only looking at what the mind thinks is your best interest—you will always be drawn to the things that have emotional attachments. I am proposing that you take a holistic approach by including the body in your decision making.

Imagine that you are a scientist who is an expert on food and the body. After reviewing the ingredients and nutrients of a frosted cupcake, noting the level of refined sugar and flour will spike your blood sugar as you digest it. Also noting the high load of refined carbohydrates and fat—remember, you are a scientist trained to do what is best for the body—how would you assess the cupcake?

When you take away the emotional attachment that drives the mind towards the cupcake and view it from a less emotional place, you may find that the desire the mind has for the cupcake is not in the best interest of the body (or the mind!). You may notice that the word *deserve* takes on a different meaning. It does not hold as much weight in convincing you as before. You may begin to perceive the idea of you *deserving* a cupcake has transformed into a less agreeable statement. Your mind has just said you *deserve* this thing that will harm you. *No way is that true.* **You *deserve* to be filled with love, abundance, and foods that nurture and nourish the body.**

Why would the mind try to convince you that you deserve something that is not in your best interest? That is an entire book in itself. What I wanted to bring to your attention is that these desires that we hold are sometimes creations of the mind that are not in our best interest. They are relics from memories of the past. There is nothing wrong or bad about having them. They are what they are.

Where we can move towards empowering ourselves right now is to see clearly our habits and behaviors and bring awareness to whether they support optimal health and development or not.

Living in the present moment also looks like a mind free of comparisons or judgments (of yourself or others). You stop worrying about what others have and start noticing what is right in front of you. You begin to see the small, beautiful details of life—the warmth of the sun, the breeze on your face, the joy of catching a ride at the perfect time. These beautiful details stimulate feelings of gratitude.

> *Gratitude shifts your focus from what is missing to what is already here.*

It is also a huge mindset shift. You begin to see life differently. Instead of asking,

"*Why is this happening to me?*"

you can ask,

"*How can this work for me?*"

This small shift in perspective can change everything. Gratitude helps you recognize the good in every situation, even when things do not go as planned. It teaches you to appreciate not just the big wins, but also the small moments—the beauty of nature, the convenience of ordering online, or the kindness of a stranger.

Gratitude may also teach you the comfort of fully expressing anger, grief, or any other emotion you are feeling. Emotions are potential teachers. You might be grateful for the emotions themselves and how they release physical or emotional tension from the body. Also, many people are taught to hold on to emotions and internalize them. Crying or expressing anger is not deemed to be acceptable in some situations. To be fully self-expressed is to be fully empowered.

This is what Reiki teaches us—to cultivate gratitude for everything, including ourselves. It helps us see the world as a place full of possibility, where we can manifest extraordinary results by being present. With gratitude, the fear of failure fades, and you find joy in simply being who you are. You begin to understand that each of us is unique, beautiful, and created by the divine. When you embrace this truth, you can watch your life transform.

Living in gratitude is not about how others see you; it is about realizing your own worth and beauty, exactly as you are. When you master this understanding, everything in your life changes for the better.

Key Points Summary:

Being Present: Living in gratitude means being fully present, appreciating what you have, and acknowledging the abundance around you. This mindset fosters joy and attracts positive experiences and opportunities.

Minimize Social Media: Social media often erodes gratitude by encouraging comparison, leading to feelings of inadequacy. This creates a negative cycle of self-judgment, diminishing your self-worth and limiting life choices.

Mindset: A "lack" mindset can influence actions, reinforcing beliefs that certain things are undeserved or unattainable. For instance, internalized feelings of inadequacy can hinder you from pursuing fulfilling experiences or opportunities.

Key Points Summary Continued:

Rationalizing a Want or Need: The concept of "deserving" often acts as a psychological permission slip, rationalizing wants or needs, which can sometimes misalign with what is genuinely beneficial for the body or mind.

Emotionally Driven Habits: Desires driven by emotional attachments or habits may not serve in your best interests. For example, associating hard work with a sugary reward like a cupcake may stem from habit, not necessarily from what nurtures the body.

Benefit the Body: Adopting a holistic view that includes the body's well-being when making decisions helps discern between desires that genuinely serve health and those that are emotional reflexes.

Finding a New Perspective: Gratitude fosters a shift in mindset, prompting questions like *"How can this work for me?"* rather than "Why is this happening to me?" This perspective helps enhance both resilience and appreciation.

Value All Emotions: Embracing gratitude involves valuing all emotions, including challenging ones like grief or anger, as they can be insightful and release stored tensions. Expressing emotions authentically is a form of self-empowerment.

Reiki and Gratitude: Reiki aligns with gratitude, encouraging appreciation for yourself and life's possibilities. It reveals a world of potential where presence and self-acceptance empower personal transformation and growth by promoting a sense of intrinsic worth and beauty, freeing you from external validation and fostering a fulfilling, self-aware existence.

Chapter 7
Releasing Worry

The Power of the Present Moment

"I will not worry" is a principle of Reiki. Throughout the previous chapter I showed that *every word you say or think holds weight*. I truly believe this. Whether you say something out loud or just think it in your mind, each word affects you emotionally. That emotion can either help you harmonize, have a neutral affect or, it can trap you in feelings of fear, anger, anxiety, or stress.

Dr. Candice Pert (1997) among others discovered that emotions have a direct impact on your immune system and overall health. Traditional Chinese Medicine has, for thousands of years, believed that dysregulation of the emotions can have a destabilizing effect on the body leading to dis-ease. Now, western science is echoing the same idea. What is captivating about this topic is:

1) any emotional imbalance whether overly joyous to fearful can have a long-term impact; and,

2) if emotions lead to imbalance they can also lead to balance.

Your body sends messages all the time.

"Move the arm this way."

"Bend."

"Cough." And more.

When you are highly emotional, especially with anger or fear, the emotions have an impact on your immune system and overall health.

When you live with gratitude and attention to words and thoughts, as mentioned in the last chapter, you start looking at your emotional landscape. What you see might surprise you. And if those surprises lead you to a desire for change, one way to start releasing worry is to ask:

>   **"How is this working for me?"** instead of "Why is this happening to me?"

This shift in thinking allows you to see the world not as a series of problems but as opportunities for learning and growth. Even if you do not like what you see, this new clarity empowers you to make better choices. You can decide to walk away from situations, relationships, or environments that no longer serve you. That sense of control over your choices helps you let go of worry and fear.

Clarity Leads to Less Worry

For instance, if you find yourself in a difficult relationship or job that you realize is not working for you, you do not have to feel trapped. By looking at the situation clearly you can see how the relationship or job is working for you—and how it is not.

Because you are not using thoughts that create a sense of disempowerment (why is this happening to me) it is less likely that emotions will overly influence your ability to make a decision. In other words, in looking at the job or relationship as it is, you might find that there are valuable skills that you are learning.

You might find that you have been blinded into approaching the work or partnership by a past experience rather than the possibility or person that is directly in front of you. Being in the present means that you choose to act from a clear mind, in a thoughtful way that will likely lead you to improve your situation.

Conversely, when you are seeing the world through an emotional pallet of expectation and assumption you tend to have stronger reactions to statements and actions. These reactions may be out of proportion to what is actually occurring.

For example, when you are buried in emotion and a normal email about a project comes in you may be enmeshed in too strong of an excited energy state to get started. Equally, you may spiral into fear about the workload and feel a sense of catastrophe coming. It all depends on past experiences.

There are many different ways that you might respond to the news of the project. What is important to note is that in each reaction, you are guided by your emotions and your previous experiences.

Sometimes you might impose the experience of a previous project onto this new project. In that case you run the danger of not seeing the project as it is. You are influenced by previous experiences both good and bad. This will, in turn, influence the nature of the dedication to this new project as you may bring past expectations and grievances to your new work.

To see the project as it is without attaching past expectations and grievances allows you to release any worry.

Recognizing that you are not in the present moment gives you the power to stop and recenter to being in the present, the now, and the communication that is taking place. From this awareness you may then observe if your reactions are meaningful or if they are based on unexpressed expectations and assumptions and leading to worry.

Awareness might not happen immediately, but knowing you have the ability to change your situation brings a sense of peace. You are no longer worried because you know you hold the power to make a shift whenever you are ready. Let us look at being present in more detail.

Stay Present to Avoid Worry

Worry pulls you out of the present moment. When you worry, your mind is either stuck in the future or the past. You might stress about what "could" happen in the future, asking yourself, "What if X goes wrong?"

Or you might dwell on something from the past, replaying scenarios in your head and wondering, "What if they think badly of me?"

But the truth is, you cannot control the future. It will unfold in its own time, regardless of how much you worry.

So why worry?

If you trust that everything is working out for you—whether it is a life lesson or something else—then anything can be fixed.

When you worry about the past, you are usually making assumptions based on your perspective. We all do this. After all, you can only see and understand the world from your perspective.

Finding Your Perspective

Back in 2008, a journalist friend in Macao told me the way she helped students understand multiple perspectives needed for reporting and life.

I have since heard this same example used by others—it is powerful—and I do not know where it originated. I will share it as I remember.

Imagine you are on assignment to cover a building on fire. The safest place to report from is in the 5 story building across the street to the one going up in smoke.

Journalists flooded the building to report on the story. The only places left for you to set up and report from are limited. You quickly note that the right side of the building is to the east and the left side to the west. You are standing on the third floor facing the west side of the building where there are plumes of smoke so thick nothing more than seven feet in front of you is visible.

You report what you see and experience. The journalist on the fifth floor sees the building's roof collapse. The journalists on the first floor see fire creeping up the walls and everything glowing with heat. Everyone sees and reports on something different.

Who is right? Who has given the most accurate report?

There is no right. There is no wrong or more accurate. There is interpretation and perspective.

Assumptions are often misleading. This creates stress over things that may not even exist. We get caught up in fear about what someone might think or how they might react, and we begin to interact with them as if our fears were already true.

Imagine this: you have been worried that someone is upset with you over something. When you finally talk to them, you might approach the conversation feeling defensive or nervous, shy, or scared assuming the other person is angry or disappointed. But in reality, they might not feel that way at all. And if they sense your fear, hesitation, or nervous energy, they might react in frustration, even though there was no issue to begin with.

Worry may create a problem that did not exist.

Dr. Mikao Usui may have understood this about the human mind because he was also a Buddhist practitioner. In Buddhism, there is a practice of understanding how the mind works and how it shapes our perception of reality. We are all influenced by our conditioning—our culture, our families, schools, and the media we consume.

Our conditioning helps us to understand how to successfully live and work in society. This is neither good nor bad. This conditioning forms the way we see the world, and it is important to recognize that as we share common values and beliefs (conditioning) **everyone also has their own unique way to see and interact with the world.**

When you understand this, it becomes easier to forgive yourself and others. You realize that people act based on their conditioning or worldview. If that view is very different from yours it is easy to see how misunderstandings may occur. This awareness helps you respond with more compassion, gratitude, and unconditional love, both toward yourself and others. Instead of holding onto grudges or worry, you begin to let go of emotional reactions.

When you release worry, you regain your sense of peace. You are no longer giving power to external situations or people to dictate your emotional state. Instead, you maintain control over your reactions, your thoughts, and your well-being.

By practicing the Reiki principle of *I will not worry*, you empower yourself to live with a calm mind and a peaceful heart, trusting that you have the ability to handle whatever life brings your way.

It takes a lot of dedicated practice and work to see yourself and your bias clearly. This is not a bad thing, most of us understand conceptually that our reality and perception is only one way to see the world. Our way to see the world. Time, kindness, curiosity, and humor help you to begin to pause and ask yourself during an interaction if your way is the only way to interpret or see what is happening.

Here are some reflection questions you might use when you notice yourself feeling emotional about an interaction or making assumptions about someone that may not be true.

Reflection questions for "I will not worry":

- What was it that activated me about our interaction?

- Is this based on an assumption? (This is often "yes" if I have not clarified what they were saying during the conversation.)

- Am I seeing this person clearly or am I projecting an intention or emotion on them?

- If I am projecting, how often do I do this?

- Where and when did I start projecting onto them?

- Are there any examples of times when I was wrong about their intentions?

- What is the gap between how I want to be treated and how they are treating me?

- Is there a gap between how they might want to be treated and how I am treating them?

- How can I lovingly construct a bridge over this gap?

- Am I attached to my perspective?

- How can I see what has occurred from another perspective?

Again, as you work through these questions and practice remember: time, kindness, curiosity, and humor help you question if your way is the only way to interpret or see what is happening.

Key Points Summary:

Reiki Principle: "I will not worry" encourages mental clarity and emotional balance, impacting health and well-being positively.

Power of Words and Thoughts: Every word, spoken or thought, affects emotional states, potentially leading to balance or imbalance. Emotions, according to both western science and Traditional Chinese Medicine, influence the immune system and overall health.

Shift in Perspective: Changing from "Why is this happening to me?" to "How is this working for me?" promotes a proactive approach, allowing you to view challenges as opportunities and make empowered choices.

Key Points Summary continued:

Present-Moment Awareness: Worry pulls the mind into the past or future, causing stress and diminishing the power of present action. Staying present helps to manage reactions with clarity rather than assumptions based on past experiences or fears.

Self-Reflection Practices: Reflection questions help identify emotional activations and assumptions in interactions, aiding in mindful responses rather than reactive ones. Practicing self-reflection builds compassion and releases emotional baggage, fostering peace and calm.

Empowerment through Letting Go of Worry: Practicing non-worry restores peace by focusing on controlling reactions rather than situations, allowing for a balanced and self-empowered approach to life.

Chapter 8

Releasing Anger

Letting Go of Suffering

The third principle of Reiki, "I will not anger," teaches us the importance of managing our emotions, especially when we feel frustrated or upset. One of my Reiki teachers, Steven Clasper, once said that anger is often a sign of guilt or a lack of acceptance of a situation or person.

This idea resonated with me deeply, especially when I reflected on my frustrations with Atlanta traffic. I expect to be able to drive through Atlanta with little traffic. Maybe in 1998. Now? There is no way. And yet, I still hold on to this idea. This expectation is unreasonable. Not being willing to see that Atlanta traffic is what it is creates the perfect recipe for anger. Watching people yell, scream, and act up in their cars shows me that I am not the only one living in the delusion that driving in Atlanta (or wherever you live) *should* be easy.

While I meant the example to have some humor, I have seen road rage that transformed lovely people into monsters with sometimes fatal results. How can it be that someone would get so overcome by anger and rage that harm seems appropriate? Harm is never appropriate.

"Turn the other cheek."

"Do no harm."

These statements express thoughts that are shared across cultures and hold an inherent meaning that you are in the present, aware of your feelings. Cheek turning can only happen if you know and are in control of your emotional temperature.

Driving is only *one* of the areas in our daily lives where we hold expectations. Many of these expectations revolve around our concept of time. When things take too long, frustration arises. From buying items at a store or restaurant, to people returning communications, to traveling from point A to point B.

Think of something that occurred this week where you became frustrated because it took too long or moved too slow.

- What if time had not been a concern during the interaction?

- Would you have felt the same level of frustration?

- Does frustration lead to anger?

Expectations also involve concepts of communication.

We may have a different style of communication than another person which leads to misunderstandings. For example, my thinking style is abstract random. What that means is that I will look at an apple on the plate of the person I am eating lunch with. That will remind me of a Halloween where we bobbed for apples, which will remind me of a person that was there that I have not seen in a long time and their dog. This will remind me that I have been wanting to adopt a dog and I might ask the person who was just talking about a football match how much time per week I would have to invest in walking a dog. In their mind, we were talking about sports and there was just a temporary lull in the conversation. In my mind, the story was completed and I began a new topic about dogs. If this person does not know me well they might think I was not listening to them and get annoyed.

This is just one of many examples of the beauty and treachery of communication. All the persons who are taking part of the communication perceive the communication happening in a certain way. When one of the group or pair says something in a way that does not make sense, many times we assume something about that communication and person rather than asking for clarification or summarizing what we understood from the context. When we assume, miscommunication arises and can become problematic, inviting frustration and anger to arise. The easiest way to alleviate miscommunication is to confirm your understanding of what someone has said.

"What I hear you saying is..(summarize the key point). Is that correct?"

Then, give them the opportunity to clarify their intended meaning.

Expectations of how something *should* be or occur
creates suffering.

Releasing anger does not mean you ignore a situation or pretend everything is fine. It simply means you choose not to let your emotional reaction control you. You can accept that something is happening or that someone is acting in a certain way, but still look for solutions or changes when needed. Take, for example, Atlanta traffic. It is inevitable that I will get stuck in traffic at some point. *Inevitable.*

To minimize my exposure, I leave early to get to an appointment so that if I hit the dreaded traffic I do not hold stress about being late. Apps will show me where there are traffic jams to avoid. I bring work, a book, podcast or make a list of people I would love to connect with during the extra time when I am early or if I stay late to avoid rush hour. When I am stuck, I sing mantras to relax me. Mantras are repeated words or phrases that may help regulate your nervous system. While the words themselves feel beautiful to say, there is something else very interesting going on. James Nestor presented a powerful practice that Dr. Richard Brown of Columbia University in his book, *Breath*. One called "Coherent Breathing" is done by deepening your breath to a 5/5 or 6/6 intake and exhale. In other words, you breath in for five seconds and exhale for five seconds. This has been scientifically shown to assist in regulating the nervous system and chanting many mantras like Om Hrim Namah Shivaya or Nam-myoho-renge-kyo (Tina Turner's chant) or Christian breath prayers will help you to reach this breath pattern (Nestor, 2020).

What I have described above are invitations to help you stay in the present: Aware of yourself, the other person, the different situations, and perspectives that might impact your experience. These actions will help you feel comfortable to enjoy the present moment rather than being in the emotion of anger or frustration.

Anger and grudges only harm you. They do not harm the person you are holding them against.

Living in the present moment helps you release the weight of your emotional history. You start to see people as they are *now*, not as they were in the past. For example, you might have a friend or family member who frustrates you—maybe they take too much of your time or seem to not care. When you recognize you hold an assumption about someone that emotionally activates you, it is first an invitation to look at why their actions or inactions bother you. This reflection, in turn, allows you to observe (without judgment) if it is activating some aspect of yourself that you are uncomfortable with. In other words, a hidden side of your personality that you do not like about yourself.

If you recognize that your frustration is based on your own beliefs and assumptions, you can step back from the emotional reaction. As your emotional response softens, you might find that the relationship begins to shift as well. Often, when you act towards another based on a belief or assumption which is based on previous interactions there is no opening for you to see any changes that might have been made based on where life has led them.

By not reacting out of anger or frustration, you can approach the person with more understanding and communicate through listening and observing what they say and do before reacting. This deep listening allows you to pause to ask questions and confirm what is meant before assumptions may be made. Keeping your conversations clear and present.

Speaking of clear and present, how does Reiki help with the assumptions and expectations about traffic I previously mentioned?

Before I started practicing Reiki, when a car cut me off by pulling right in front of me at a stop light, blocking my turn into the parking area at work, I would yell in my car, "How rude!" My mind immediately went into frustration and anger. Incensed, I was about to spiral into thoughts of annoyance. My mind was blocked from balance.

The other day, a red car pulled right in front of me, inches away from knocking off my bumper. My mind jumped to anger. But the music from the car next to me said, "unblock your mind." I started laughing. Rather than a flood of feelings about the red car's driver, I regained my balance. It also reminded me to slow down. There was no need to rush when I could enjoy the experience of being in the car, windows down, on a beautiful day. And I reflected that the beautiful shiny red car that was blocking where I wanted to be could be a metaphor for any number of "shiny" things in my life that were pulling focus away from being present.

The Reiki principle, Release Anger, invites you to let go of these expectations. There is no single right way to handle situations that are influenced by our expectations, but there are choices. The first and highly helpful choice is to recognize when you feel anger and ask,

"What is the expectation I have here?"

If it is difficult to identify the expectation, I invite you to consider *should*. If you hear yourself saying *should* this is an expectation. The traffic in Atlanta (Los Angeles, London, Shanghai, etc.) with wrecks, too many cars on the roads, and overly slow or fast drivers, should not be so difficult to drive through. It is not. Thinking the traffic *should* be easy is not accepting the reality of the situation.

If I base my expectation on reality, I know there will be traffic. I will then come up with some approaches to managing my expectations about the traffic and my time.

- What is it that angers you currently?

- What is the lack of acceptance, expectation or assumption behind the anger? Why does it make you angry?

- Like my strategies for traffic, what are the approaches you can take to manage your experience of the thing that makes you angry right now?

- When you accept things for the way that they are, what are all the ways that you might change the way you approach it?

Another example of unfilled expectations and miscommunication causing anger and upset may be giving a gift to someone and expecting that they will think and respond in a certain way. When I lived in

Macao, a friend brought me a beautiful batik fabric from Indonesia. It was incredible. To liven up my office and create joy whenever I entered it, I put the fabric on my chair. One day, I came back to my office and the fabric was gone. The friend had taken it back. I walked over to his office to ask why. He said I was not using the gift correctly. His expectation—what I should do—had created so much anger for him over the course of a month at how I was using the material that he took it back. Communicating that the fabric had a happy emotional meaning for me and that it felt like a big splash of joy he gave the fabric back. We recovered and twelve years later, I still feel joy when looking at the fabric.

Some approaches work for certain people, and others do not. What matters is finding the method that helps you accept what is and release what you feel guilt or shame about. By accepting a situation for what it is, you will notice that your frustration and annoyance begin to fade.

When you manage anger, you make clearer decisions and see things from a broader perspective. Anger narrows your vision, making it hard to see options and solutions. But when you approach life with contentment, ease, and gratitude, you open up to understanding different viewpoints.

In Reiki, this calm state allows energy to flow freely, making us better practitioners. I am not willing to hold onto anger to impact my day, especially if it can stop me from being the calm and effective Reiki channel I want to be. That is why Dr. Usui emphasized not letting anger control you. Staying grounded in acceptance lets you channel Reiki more effectively and appreciate the lessons that even situations or people you find frustrating can teach you.

Key Points Summary:

Anger and Expectations: The third Reiki principle, "I will not anger," teaches managing emotions by examining underlying expectations or lack of acceptance, which often cause frustration and anger.

Unrealistic Expectations: Using Atlanta (or any!) traffic as an example, the text explores how unrealistic expectations (like expecting smooth traffic) can lead to anger. Acceptance of reality helps reduce frustration.

Communication: Miscommunication can also create anger, especially when people have different communication styles. Clarifying and checking understanding can prevent assumptions and reduce frustration.

Acceptance of Reality: Recognizing and releasing unrealistic expectations allows you to respond to situations calmly.

Being Present: You are encouraged to pause to appreciate the present moment, even in difficult or inconvenient situations, by letting go of unnecessary expectations.

Reflection and Self-Questioning: The practice of asking questions like, "What expectation is driving my anger?" helps identify and release the root cause of anger.

Embracing Calmness: By managing anger and releasing control, you gain clarity and broader perspectives. This shift not only improves your well-being but also makes you as a Reiki practitioner more effective by allowing energy to flow freely.

Learning from Frustration: Frustrating situations offer lessons in acceptance and patience, enhancing your ability to handle similar challenges gracefully in the future.

Chapter 9

Working Honestly

Integrity Is the Key

M any years of my life were spent working dishonestly. Did that catch your attention? I meant it to because you too may be working dishonestly without even realizing it.

Before we go further, a clarification.

When we talk about working honestly, it is easy to think it just means being a good person—someone who does not lie, cheat, or steal, and who does their job well. I believe that you probably fit into this description. You may be kind, thoughtful, telling the truth and acting honorably around your place of work.

The deeper meaning of working honestly is about acting with integrity. Integrity means living and working in a way that reflects your true self. It is not just about being honest with others—it is about being honest with yourself. Whatever work you do, whether it is schoolwork, a job, or a hobby, should be done with respect for yourself and others. Approach your work with pride, because only you can bring your unique skills and gifts to it. Acting in this way, regardless of the job, elevates your experience in this world.

Think about it this way: maybe you have a knack for making people feel seen and appreciated when you greet them. A friend of mine brought this talent to a coffee shop. He greeted customers with such care, attention, and presence that he elevated people. An interaction with him would positively impact their day. This friend stayed present throughout his shift regardless of how others treated him because he understands the importance of being authentic, kind, and uplifting.

Whatever your talents are, when you work with integrity, you offer these gifts to the world, and in doing so, you feel joy and satisfaction. It does not matter what kind of work or activity you are doing, but how you are interacting with the world.

At the beginning of the chapter, I shared how I did not realize I was far from doing the work I was meant to be doing. It turns out that while teaching is the work that I am meant to be doing, I was teaching the wrong thing. Teaching is something that I am good at and enjoy. When I started teaching something aligned with my purpose, like how to play the gongs or Reiki, I was in my element and the world felt right.

For many years I did not know what I was meant to be doing. Thus, my work felt frustrating. The inner fire was not there. Once I started aligning my teaching with my purpose, I could take a risk on building a business that I love.

Do any of the previous statements ring true for you?

If so, I offer the following questions to excavate your skills, talents, and desires.

- What are interactions (plants, animals, people) that light me up?

- What did I want to do when I was five?

- What about my five-year-old dreams still captivate me?

- What did I want to do when I was 10? 15? 20? 25?

- What about those dreams still captivate me?

- Who was I going to be in those dreams then?

- Do I still wish to be that person?

- If so, what characteristics and behaviors would that person have?

- If not, what are the characteristics and behaviors of the person you wish to be?

- What is a small change that you could make today to be more like that person?

This second set of questions helped me plan how to move careers. Each job has the potential to teach us how to do or not to do things. When you can see how the work you are currently engaged in supports the overall arc of your development towards what you are meant to do, expansiveness opens up to possibilities as your thoughts about the purpose and impact of your work. This leads to joy and happiness.

- What do I really dislike doing?

- If I am currently doing something I dislike, what can I find in what I dislike that is a skill set I am learning?

- Is my dislike based on my perception of something that may not be entirely true? If so, how can I shift my thinking about what I dislike?

- If I am not doing something I dislike, how can I keep things this way?

- How does my current job support me?

- Financially?

- Emotionally?

- Physically?

- What are all the possible ways I can build on that support?

Society does not always value all gifts equally. We often see celebrities, athletes, or entertainers being celebrated, while teachers, nurses, or plumbers, to name a few—jobs that are essential to our community—do not get the same recognition. The world sometimes sends the message that if you are not rich or famous, your work does not matter.

This is not true.

To the people that my friend elevates at the coffee shop, he is the most important part of their day. The teachers who bring students out of their shells, they matter very much. You never know how your interaction with someone shifts the course of their life. But this Reiki principle, Work Honestly, reminds us that material success does not equal integrity. You can have money or fame and still feel unfulfilled if you are not living and working in a way that is true to who you are.

You can tell if you are working with integrity by how you feel about your work.

- Do you feel inspired and energized by what you do a majority of the time?

- Does it fit your personality and likes?

- Do you feel claustrophobic at your job?

- Do you feel that you have a purpose?

If your work reflects your personality, values, and skills, you are probably working with at least partial integrity as I was a teacher. This does not mean you will be doing this forever, but it shows you are in a place where you can grow and thrive right now and you develop the expertise, skills, and experience necessary to transition into what you are meant to do.

On the other hand, if you are constantly miserable, it is a sign that something is off.

If you feel out of place in your work or life, ask yourself:

"Where do I feel happy, engaged, and fulfilled?"

Maybe you enjoy interacting with people, but your job keeps you isolated. That is a mismatch. You might need to switch roles at your current job or even find a new one that allows you to be more social.

Being honest with yourself requires looking at your life clearly. Often, we judge ourselves based on what we think we *should* be doing, influenced by those around us or what we see in the media. But Reiki teaches us to connect with love and heart to see ourselves more clearly. By doing so, we can live with integrity, accept life as it is, and still work toward change.

Working honestly means doing work that reflects who you truly are. When you do, you feel more alive, fulfilled, and ready to give your best to the world around you.

Key Points Summary:

Align Work with True Self: Working honestly goes beyond traditional concepts of honesty; it means aligning your work with your true self. Working with integrity means staying true to your personality and values, allowing for growth and transition to more purposeful work.

Integrity and Authenticity: Integrity in work is about bringing your unique gifts to your role, regardless of the type of work. Living authentically and in alignment with purpose can lead to fulfillment, joy, and satisfaction in your work.

Purpose: Discovering purpose may involve reflecting on childhood interests, current passions, and dislikes to identify fulfilling paths.

Work as Service: Society often undervalues certain professions, but each role has the potential to positively impact others' lives. Material success does not equate to integrity; true fulfillment comes from work that resonates with personal values and passions.

Feelings as a Barometer: Assessing your feelings about work can indicate alignment with integrity; feelings of inspiration and energy suggest alignment, while constant misery signals a need for change.

Reiki and Honesty: Reiki encourages self-reflection and acceptance, helping you to see clearly what truly resonates, beyond societal expectations or external judgments.

Chapter 10

Honoring Others

We Are Mirrors for Each Other

Others act as mirrors for you, reflecting aspects of yourself back to you. This teaches you about who you are and how you interact with the world. I experienced this firsthand when I was giving a teacher training workshop in Ukraine. I had a master's degree and extensive experience, but I felt insecure, like I was not supposed to be leading the training. One of the men in the group challenged me constantly by questioning everything I said. At first, I got frustrated and angry, feeling like I was not respected for my expertise.

Mid presentation, I paused and reflected. First, I realized that I was feeling attacked because I did not respect my own experience and knowledge. This may have impacted the way that I put the materials together. Second, I realized that he may not have known about my background.

I was assuming he would take me at face value as an expert. This reflection took thirty seconds. As I stood with all eyes on me, I thought, "What can I learn from this? What do his questions tell me he needs to feel intellectually satisfied?" I adjusted my presentation on the spot. Then, when I got back to the hotel, I adjusted it for the remainder of the week.

Over dinner I reflected on how I had been making assumptions about how the material should be delivered and how I should be treated. He had also made assumptions. My reactions to him were based on my own insecurities and experiences rather than other possible interpretations. It does not matter that I will never know his intentions. What matters is that he, through our interaction, showed me where there was potential for growth in myself and my approach. He exposed areas that were to be healed.

In community, there is a potential to help each other grow and become our best selves. There are a many simple ways to honor those around us. A thank you to family members, acknowledgments for help and fixing things, a thank you to a cashier, statements of appreciations for....

What are some of the ways you can honor those at home and those around you as you go about your day?

Everyone has something to offer, no matter what their age or experience. By honoring others, especially those who trigger strong emotions in us, we are honoring ourselves. They are showing us something about ourselves that, through addressing, we might have more ease and peace in our lives.

Once we accept those parts of ourselves, we often find that those same people no longer bother us in the same way. By seeing ourselves clearly, we can celebrate who we are, and this allows us to celebrate others too.

By honoring others we build community, we help support others and ourselves, we respect those around us who are working hard - doing the best with the capacities they have at this time. And respect our teachers, leaders, volunteers, workers, etc. for what they've contributed and how much it can make a difference in our lives. Just a little bit of kindness to others every opportunity we have.

Honoring Others is the last of the five practices that Dr. Usui used as guidelines. When taken together, they form an incredible foundation for living a joyful, thriving, and lovingly compassionate life.

In the following chapter, you will find the steps to build a foundation for any energetic practice you wish to pursue. If you take nothing else from this book, working with these principles on a daily basis has the possibility to bring you greater happiness and joy by staying in the present moment.

This is not to say that by practicing the principles everything will immediately be in alignment. It will not. Nor will change occur overnight and for good.

Each day is continual dedication to the practices. Some days will be stellar. Other days, weeks, months, and years will breeze by with some of the practices discontinued. Suffering and disharmony may arise because of loss of practice. Even so, you will never go back to where you were before you dropped the practice. Luckily, you can always restart the practice and bring yourself back into harmony.

Practice is ongoing. There is no perfect. Fall out of practice and begin again the next day.

Just today, don't worry about tomorrow.

Just today you can do that thing.

Then, see if you want to continue tomorrow.

Key Point Summary:

Self-Reflection Through Others: Interactions with others act as mirrors, reflecting parts of yourself that may need growth or healing. I share my experience in Ukraine where a challenging participant helped reveal my own insecurities and assumptions, leading to personal growth and adjustment.

Learning from Triggers: Strong emotions triggered by others offer insights into areas needing acceptance within yourself. By addressing these reactions, you can foster inner peace and better relationships.

Building Community through Respect: Honoring and respecting others, especially those who challenge you, strengthens community and nurtures mutual growth. Kindness and respect for everyone, regardless of role or experience, enriches your life and theirs.

The Practice of Honoring in Reiki: Honoring Others is the final of the five Reiki principles by Dr. Usui, providing a foundation for a compassionate and joyful life. Practicing these principles can bring happiness by keeping you grounded in the present.

Commitment to Practice: These principles are not a one-time solution but require daily, ongoing dedication. Practicing them can be inconsistent, yet returning to them helps restore harmony. The guidance is to take it "just today," without stressing about long-term perfection.

Chapter 11
How Do You Start an Energetic Practice?

Five Easy Steps

R eiki is available to you when you are ready. If you want to explore different practices before committing to studying Reiki as a practitioner, the following part of the book will assist you in developing a meaningful energetic practice.

An energetic practice helps you harmonize your body to its highest potential. As you harmonize yourself you will find resonance (matching vibration) with the world around you. This state feels beautiful. You will notice more synchronicities occurring in your life. Now, do not get me wrong, I am not saying that you will be in a state of bliss all day every day. You and I are creatures of a changeable and emotionally dynamic world. Sadness, grief, anger still occur.

And yet, with Reiki and a stable energetic practice, you may recognize, process, and release emotions from the body and mind at a greater pace and with less difficulty than without Reiki. For example, it is the difference between getting stuck in anger while I am in traffic and carrying it like a cloak, influencing my entire day or letting anger go.

I *am* angry versus I *feel* angry.

If I *am* angry, I believe myself to be consumed by the emotion. It defines who I am at that given moment in time because I personally associate with it. If I *feel* anger, anger does not define who I am. Feeling an emotion means that you are not the emotion. Anger is identified as a feeling. Feelings pass. This means that anger will pass when a new emotion arises. This gives me space to feel the emotion and let it pass without carrying it longer than necessary.

At the end of each practitioner's chapter they offer an energetic practice that helps them move towards harmony and is something you could start today. These practices may help you to develop the innate capacities that you already possess. What is powerful about the stories in this book is that every person has a different need for harmony in the body and mind. Some you will connect with. As you do the practices suggested, you will find yourself moving towards greater awareness of the present.

Reiki will activate your inner healer to address any imbalances. Your inner healer is an intelligence, a consciousness, within your body that can guide, protect, and help you heal. Your inner healer is re-activated and re-develops the capacity to process, release, and transform pain and stress from your past traumatic experiences, through energetic healing practices. This is self-healing. This inner healer communicates through your subconscious and conscious mind. By slowing down and allowing space and time every day to connect with the inner healer, it will teach you how to work towards harmonizing yourself and others.

To slow down and create an environment that fosters this type of communication is the practice we are inviting you to explore. Since every person approaches energetic work in a way that resonates with them, everyone's practice will be distinct in nature, time, and space. However, there are some core or foundational steps.

Step 1: Choose a Practice That Resonates with You

The authors of this book share several different types of practices. Whether it is building an altar, Reiki, yoga, or sound meditation, start your own practice with what appeals to you. If you are unsure where to begin, consider starting at the beginning with the practice Alice offers. Try it for a week and keep a journal or notes about what you observe. Then, continue on to Anthony's practice for a week. Try each practitioner's offering for a period of time that works for you. Adapt and adjust the practices as you go so that they begin to feel like home to you. Mix and match them until you have found something that feels just right for now.

Another way to explore is to sign up for classes on energy practice. Learn to play singing bowls, chant mantras, or a gong, for example.

What is interesting about energetic work is that as you evolve, change, and grow, your practice will too! In the same way you move grade after grade through school towards graduation, as you develop skills with energy work, different types of modalities will resonate with you. You may start with oracle cards or runes then transition to sound or vice versa. There is nothing but boundless possibility.

Step 2: Set an Intention

All practitioners start with an intention for the practice or work they are doing. This helps guide the experience and gives the energy direction. Intentions are one of the foundations to any energetic practice.

Here is what an intention is: An intention is a clear, specific goal or desired outcome that you focus on achieving. It is setting a target or a purpose for your actions. Without a target or purpose it is easy to lose your momentum and way. It helps you stay focused on what you want to achieve and guides your conscious and subconscious energy toward that goal.

I intend to....

Before you begin your daily practice, set a clear intention. To do so, ask yourself, "What do I hope to achieve or feel through this practice?"

Sometimes the result you are looking for is difficult to put into words. In that case, you can either dig a little deeper or set a more general intention like,

> "*I intend to use this practice to bring my body, mind, emotions, and spirit into harmony and balance for my highest good.*"

Here is why this intention works:

1. Specific:

What It Is: This intention is about using *a specific practice* (such as meditation, Reiki, or any other healing method) *to achieve* harmony and balance in various aspects of oneself: body, mind, emotions, and spirit.

Why It Is Important: Defining the intention clarifies that the goal is to achieve overall well-being and balance. It sets a clear purpose for why the practice is being undertaken.

2. Clarity:

What It Is: The intention is to bring "body, mind, emotions, and spirit" into "harmony and balance."

Why It Is Important: This part of the intention is clear in terms of *what is being sought*—balance and harmony across multiple aspects of oneself. It helps in understanding that the goal is holistic, addressing various dimensions of well-being.

3. Positivity:

What It Is: The intention is framed positively, *focusing on achieving* harmony and balance rather than avoiding something negative.

Why It Is Important: Positive framing makes the intention more inspiring and motivating. It encourages a focus on the desired outcome (balance and harmony) rather than the problems or imbalances.

4. Believability:

What It Is: The intention *assumes that achieving* harmony and balance through the practice *is possible and realistic*.

Why It Is Important: For the intention to be effective, it needs to be achievable. The belief that harmony and balance can be attained through the practice reinforces commitment and motivation.

5. Emotion:

What It Is: The intention *connects to a deep desire* for well-being and personal growth.

Why It Is Important: Emotional connection adds depth and significance to the intention. It enhances motivation by aligning the practice with personal values and desires for improvement.

6. Action:

What It Is: *Using the practice as a tool* to bring about the desired balance.

Why It Is Important: The intention includes taking action (engaging in the practice) to achieve the goal. Without action, the intention remains just a wish. The practice itself becomes the means through which balance and harmony are pursued.

Reflection plays an important part of an energetic practice. Reflecting on how well the practice is contributing to harmony and balance helps in refining the approach for better results. These are the core reflective questions that might be asked:

- How did you feel physically?

- Did you notice any changes in your body (shoulders loosening, stomach not as tense)? Emotionally?

- You might also like to look at how successful you felt in completing the practice. What did you like? What would you do differently next time (maybe choosing different words or visualizations)?

- What question do you still have that you might find answers to online? By taking a class with a qualified professional?

Intentions are *everything* in the world of energetic practice. Another aspect that is very important is creating a routine.

Step 3: Create a Routine

Consistency is key. Start small by dedicating 5-10 minutes each day to your chosen practice. Whether it is sitting quietly and focusing on your breath, attending a yoga class, or journaling, regular practice allows your body and mind to adjust to the energetic shifts you are creating.

Step 4: Journal Your Experience

As many of my clients have shared, keeping a journal of your experiences can be transformational. Write about your practice, your emotions, and how your body feels after each session. Focus especially on moments when you feel uplifted or deeply connected. These are moments of high vibration, and noticing these helps you align your energy. More about this practice can be found in the chapter, *White-Knuckled with Anxiety*.

Step 5: Allow for Authentic Expression

It is important to be honest about what comes up during your practice, whether it is joy or discomfort. While journaling, avoid reactivating past traumas by focusing on your current emotions and the process of releasing them rather than dwelling on the pain itself.

As you will notice in the stories and practices over the next couple of chapters, each one of us is beautifully unique and responds to energy work in a different way. Therefore, listen to your inner self as you read. It will guide you to what feels right for your body, mind, and spirit.

By following these steps, you can create a strong foundation for your energetic practice. It is a journey of tuning in to yourself, noticing what works, and releasing what does not serve you. The goal is not perfection, but progress—one breath, one session, and one day at a time.

Now, let us explore real-life stories from various Reiki practitioners, highlighting the many ways healing is possible and how Reiki and energetic practices can transform lives.

Key Points Summary:

Starting with Energy Practices: You are encouraged to explore different energetic practices to find personal resonance. This practice may harmonize the body, though it will not eliminate all challenges or difficult emotions.

Emotional Processing through Reiki: Reiki supports recognizing, processing, and releasing emotions, allowing a sense of flow (e.g., feeling anger rather than being consumed by anger).

Developing Awareness with Practitioner Stories: Each Reiki practitioner shares personal practices that have helped them move towards harmony. These practices may guide you in nurturing your own energetic capacities and awareness.

Steps to Begin an Energetic Practice:

- Step 1: Choose a Practice that Resonates – Experiment with various practices, adapting them to feel authentic.

- Step 2: Set an Intention – Intention guides the practice with clear, achievable, positively framed goals.

- Step 3: Create a Routine – Consistency is crucial; even 5-10 minutes a day can bring significant changes.

- Step 4: Journal Your Experiences – Track feelings and bodily responses to deepen the understanding of personal shifts.

- Step 5: Allow Authentic Expression – Reflect honestly on each practice session without dwelling on past traumas or activations.

Individualized Practice: Recognizing that each person's journey with energetic work is unique, the text encourages tuning into your inner self and evolving the practice as you grow.

Making Headway: Progress over perfection. It does not matter how fast or slow you go just as long as just today you are doing something.

Chapter 12

Creating Lovely Things: Gardening & Community

Alice Smith, MS, MBA, MGV

Taking Reiki Level 1 training with Eve was out of curiosity: *What benefits would accrue for me, and could I share this energy healing with others?*

Honestly, I didn't know much about Reiki until I tried it out in a private session with Eve. The experience of deep relaxation, release of muscle tension, and generally "feeling great!" afterwards opened my mind to learning more about the power of this gentle, loving process. When Eve offered a Traditional Usui Level 1 training course, I said, "*I'm in.*"

I knew I'd come to the right training at the right time when I read the first quote by Nikola Tesla in the course document:

> *If you want to find the secrets of the universe, think in terms of energy, frequency and vibration.*

Personally, I'd been investigating the concept that things are vibrational in our universe in works by Louise Hay and Jerry and Esther Hicks. It appeared the foundational principle of Reiki, universal life force energy, was complementary to other works that made sense to me and also worked for me.

Then the lead statement from the training manual: "It [Reiki] is a powerful healing process, energizing, meditative, dynamic and a balancing force of spirit, mind, emotion, and body."

If I could have access to that healing process, I thought, this could be part of my foundation of self-care for the rest of my life!

The training expanded my understanding of how Reiki awakens the chakras, unblocking and rebalancing them to flow life force energy to where it is needed and wanted. What I loved about the Reiki system was understanding that it's not about me - I'm just a simple channel for the flow of energy that can work in life-changing ways. Also, the meditations we practiced to relax and slip into a state of gratitude were easy to recall and, oh, so effective.

The training course did not end after seven hours. It included 21-days of self-practice to anchor the Reiki principles, practice the meditations, build self-confidence with hand position placements to guide the energy, and to feel the flow of energy through my hands and the energy field of my body.

During the 21-day practice after my training session, I quickly learned that the time to practice Reiki for me was before bed, that sometimes I was going to fall asleep during the breathing exercises, but that I would always wake up and finish. When I was in a deeper state of relaxation during my practice, I might fall asleep, and that was okay. Rather than tense up or try to stay alert while practicing, I learned to trust my body to know if it needed sleep and to let it happen.

Answers came quickly.

After the first week of self-practice I realized my nighttime dreams switched from dreaded repetitive nightmares of playing cards and having a stranger come into the group to kill someone, to "sweet dreams" of activities and play or even some dreamless nights. The next week I noticed the burning sensations of neuropathy in my shins were gone and I could now feel my formerly numb toes all the time. The third week I felt rebalanced, whole and complete, in body, mind, emotions and spirit.

Then came the shocker. At my appointment with my new primary care, no one (2 medical staff cross-checked each other) could hear my heart murmur. They told me there was no murmur, it wasn't there and asked, *"Why do you think you have one?"*

35 years before this office visit, I was diagnosed with a heart murmur after a bout of rheumatic fever. At all my health checks until this one the doctor would tell me that they could hear it. For years I had to take an antibiotic before each dental appointment to prevent possible strep infection growing on the compromised heart value. [FYI: This is no longer standard dental practice.]

I was also restricted from lifting heavy items, and always had to ask others for assistance even when outwardly I looked healthy enough to pick up the box. When I told Eve about the mysterious disappearance of my heart murmur she said, "Reiki." She'd provided distance Reiki with me for a year before my training with her, then I'd practiced self-Reiki for 21-days. After that at my next medical appointment. No heart murmur. Nada. Zip. Gone and it has not returned.

My Reiki "service" is to my environment and friends.

My yard is transforming.

For years I've been drawn to gardening and trying to create areas
or views from my porch that "soothe my soul." A favorite gift from
my mother-law is a small hand-drawn picture of plants entwined
with butterflies, little mammals, birds, and many of the little things
that matter most. These illustrations surround the verse, "Whatsoever
things are lovely, think on these things" (Philippians 4:8 Bible, King
James Version). I've tried to create lovely things to look at and think
on as I've developed my yard.

First, I tried to develop a few sacred spaces: areas that were calming
and felt safe; where energies from the environment rebalanced and
calmed my nervous, "let's get this done and move on" tendencies.
Since starting my Reiki practice my thinking has expanded into: "Why
not the whole yard, and what about something inside, too?" Reiki is
a universal force and has benefits to all life - people, animals, plants,
trees, even inanimate objects. Not only do I benefit, but also the
environment I'm surrounding myself with does too.

Sometimes I notice my guardian angel team is with me: with the
ease of finding things I want for the yard when I'm shopping; the
ease of cutting through sod and turning up the soil; the changing
breeze bringing a light rain shower when nothing was predicted but
I so wanted it for my plant "babies." And I say, "thank you, I'm so
grateful for...and that you're here with me." I recognize the moments
as opportunities to practice one of the five Reiki principles - Just for
today I will live in an attitude of gratitude. Grateful for the abundance
of healing, loving energy in my life.

This past August the eyewall of a hurricane passed through our
yard. A magnificent cypress tree bent and swayed, protecting the front
of our house from brutal winds from 8 a.m. when the electricity went
out until 2 p.m. A final burst of forceful wind twisted branches and

wrenched its roots from the sodden soil. The tree lay sideways, broken but still a windbreak protecting us until the storm's end. After removing the tree during yard clean up, we chose to honor it by creating a sacred circular garden in its space rather than replanting.

The new bed was filled with shrubs, perennials, vines, and ground covers that will bloom in colors representing the archangels and Celtic energies associated with ordinal positions (N,E,S,W) from spring until frost, providing spiritual energies, shelter and nourishment for the birds, bees, and butterflies.

- North: blue plumbago shrubs for Archangel Michael and a gray stone for winter solstice energies;

- East: pink climbing aster vine and weigela shrub for Ostara and spring equinox energies and green foliage for Archangel Raphael;

- South: fiery orange red blossoms of native firebush plants and coral honeysuckle vine for Litha and summer solstice energies and Archangel Uriel;

- West: white blooming Walter's viburnum and gardenia shrubs and brown pine bark mulch for Mavon and autumn equinox energies and Archangel Gabriel.

Each plant was tucked in and is frequently lovingly touched with my bare hands giving Reiki universal life force energy. All of us are thriving.

I'm still in the Reiki conversation.

Now I feel I'm living up to a much greater potential of my creative capabilities and that Reiki energy infuses all of my favorite things: gardening, leading and managing people and having them get value out of their participation whether it's book club, weeding in the community's park, or fellowship over lunch together. After the Reiki training and practice, I've opened up how I communicate and participate with others in my community. Everyone is showing up for the book club I coordinate and say each meeting, "*This is my favorite thing to do*," and "*I feel like I have a group of sisters looking out for me.*" This year I mailed everyone I knew Valentine's cards and received a stream of email messages: "*thanks for thinking of me*," and "*this will be the only Valentine card I get this year.*" Members organized lunch together after our recent meeting. They wanted to spend more time together...and there were more emails to open afterwards.

The digital clocks on the stove, in the car, and on my mobile phone show up at 1:11, 10:10, 5:55, etc. a lot these days. I didn't know what was going on so I searched the internet for the meaning of repetitive numbers. What I learned is that repetitive numbers are considered signs or messages from one's higher self and are part of opening to Spirit (a.k.a. spiritual awakening). That seemed to fit with what was going on for me. At 1:11 today I felt the need to check my phone for messages. *"Please call."* A close friend was reaching out for a trusted listener. Now when a repetitive number pops up, I touch the screen and whisper, "Thank you, Spirit. I appreciate you being here with me now." I feel comforted, loved. All's right in my world.

Spirit downloads can be trusted. Suggestions come: "slow down" when I careen around a corner of the kitchen, "be easy" when I start to chew on a concern, "things are working out'" when I open my morning pages journal and write a page of all the ways I appreciate that things working out for me, and recently, profoundly, "express your love to all around you - plants and people, too."

I am expanding my understanding. This is part of spiritual awakening. Thanks to my experiences and training, an outpouring of Reiki love energy for all around me (and for me, too) is here, always.

Alice's Reiki in the Garden Practice

Whether we realize it or not, the plants around us have an energy field. That is why you may feel calmer, at peace, or energized when you enter a garden, a nature park, or walk on a path through a forested area.

When you add a few potted plants in an area of your home, a plant energy field is available to you, and can be a relaxing, calming, soothing place where you go to meditate, practice reflective journaling, daydream, write, etc.

Regularly connect with the plant energy of nature around you, either outside or inside.

- Set an intention to give restorative, healing energy to the plants where you are: garden, park, pots in your special space at home.

- Enter the garden slowly and approach a cluster of plants. If you match your breath to your steps, you create a walking meditation. Step, breathe in. Step, breathe out. (I either use a walking stick or bend my knees to help me keep balance—find a way that works for you.)

- When you arrive at the cluster of plants, close your eyes and take 2-3 deep breaths in and out. As you breathe in, pull the air all the way down to your belly. Then observe as each lung fills with air until it reaches the back of your throat. Release. If this type of breath is uncomfortable to you, breathe as deeply as it feels relaxing. Then return to your normal breathing. Imagine roots growing down into the soil.

- When you feel centered, peaceful and ready, open yourself

to universal energy and slowly breathe as you imagine heal-ing energy flowing through your crown chakra (top of your head) throughout your body and into your hands.

- Slowly open your eyes and gently touch the leaves and blos-soms with your fingertips and palms, visualizing universal life force (love) energy flowing through your hands and to the plants.

- Say, "You are beautiful. Thank you for being here. I love you."

- Repeat, moving slowly around the garden, touching leaves and flowers.

- When finished, thank Reiki for the healing love energy for the plants and for the pollinators that visit them. May they be in harmony and balance.

- Journal about your experience: What did you notice about the tension in your body when you were around your plants? The trees? The forested area? The park? Or, concentrate on the changes you see in nature around you. What do you notice about the plants after a week of sending them loving energy? Have they grown or changed in any way?

After working 40 years with educational, healthcare and community organizations, on program development, applied research, training and mentoring employees and students, I sought out and practiced a variety of stress reduction and self-healing programs.

The programs that helped me focus, be productive, be calm, have good times with friends and family, and nourished my spirit, I kept and still practice today. The Reiki energy sessions and Level 1 training with Eve brought harmony for my body and spirit. Over time I've transformed from feeling like a "beast of burden" to feeling satisfied and free.

Now as a community volunteer, people share their concerns about work, social and financial stressors on their health and lives. I share, when appropriate, the modalities and practices that have helped me thrive with those who want less stress, more balance, more fun and more joy in their lives.

Connect with Alice on YouTube for practical gardening tips and information to help you create the garden you love at https://www.youtube.com/@gardenyay or Google @gardenyay

Chapter 13

The Energy of Reciprocity

On Healing the Land by Eve

The practice of giving back Alice speaks about in "Creating Lovely Things" is essential. Often, we go into nature to absorb its healing energy, but we forget we are a part of a cycle and have to give back as well. Balance is key in everything, and earth energy is no exception. Just as in life, if we only take and never give, our source of energy becomes depleted. Nature, too, thrives on this reciprocal exchange.

Over fifteen years ago, I traveled to Glastonbury, England, a place renowned for its healing waters, energy, and mystical qualities. At that time, I was not particularly interested in energy work, but I knew I had a connection with the spiritual world—I could feel the presence of ghosts, though I did not fully understand what was happening. The energy of Glastonbury back then was extraordinary. It was as if the land itself buzzed with life. The sensation was remarkable—a soft, light energy, like a cool breeze on a hot summer day. It felt soothing, revitalizing, and undeniably healing. The plants around me were vibrant and healthy, nourished by this palpable energy.

In July 2024 I returned to Glastonbury. From the moment I arrived, I noticed an emptiness in the energy. You know that feeling when you meet someone you know to be vibrant and full of life, but something this time just feels off? That was the sensation I got from the land. The next day, I visited a famous garden that was once lush and brimming with life, known for its healing properties. To my shock, the garden was in decline. Plants were suffering from blight and mold, and the energy of the water, once so vibrant, felt diminished.

How could such a profound change occur in just fifteen years? The answer lies in our relationship with the land. When we continuously take from the earth without giving anything back, the land becomes unable to sustain us. It is similar to over-farming, where growing the same crop year after year strips the soil of its nutrients. The same principle applies to energy. If the energy of the people living in a place, or the interactions within it, become imbalanced over time, the land's energy will shift accordingly. People have been taking the energy from Glastonbury without offering any in return. The energetic overcon-sumption is now energetically obvious. When we work with nature it has to be a two-way street.

This is not just happening in Glastonbury. It is a problem I have noticed in Decatur, where my studio is located. If you drive just an hour towards Arabia Mountain or Stone Mountain, you can feel the difference. The land there is vibrant, filled with abundant energy that is almost tangible. If you are sensitive to energy, you will feel it as a buzzing lightness or a sense of relaxation. However, the closer you get to downtown Atlanta and Decatur, the more this energy diminishes. Urban development and the high levels of stress and anxiety associated with city life seem to drain the land of its natural vitality. In some parts of the city, it feels like there is almost no energy left in the land.

Why does this matter? If the land is depleted of energy, so are we. In their book *Earthing* (2010), Clinton Ober, Stephen Sinatra, and Martin Zucker remind us that humans are composed of cells that produce an electrical charge. This is the same energy measured by EKGs and other medical tools that track our vital signs. Similarly, the earth itself produces energy, through the movements of subatomic particles called free electrons. When we walk barefoot on the ground or lie on the grass, we absorb these electrons, which help to heal and harmonize us. One of the Reiki practitioners contributing to this book, Felicia Holden, offers us a grounding practice in her chapter, *Healing Animals with Reiki*.

Alice's practice of offering Reiki to plants and the land is a beautiful way to restore balance. By sharing the loving energy of Reiki, she creates harmony between the act of taking—whether it is flowers, food, or simply the earth's energy—and the act of giving back. Reiki is not just about harmonizing people or animals; it can also be a powerful tool for healing the earth itself. When we work with nature in this way, we foster a relationship of mutual support, ensuring that both we and the land can thrive in balance and harmony.

Chapter 14

The Electricity of Reiki

Anthony Jones

A t an early age, I felt there were things beyond the physical that exist spiritually and metaphysically. What I was taught in church, for example, being burned in hellfire forever by a merciful and loving God, didn't make sense to me as I got older. That doesn't sound like a merciful and loving God, does it?

Also, how can I be born in sin for Adam's wrongdoing when the son is not responsible for the sins of the father nor is the father responsible for the sins of the son, as the Bible clearly states in Ezekiel 8:20. There are many more things that also seem to be contradictory.

This led me to reading and searching continually for the answers to the questions I had since being indoctrinated with religious teachings. Even so, metaphysics was never part of my understanding or thinking before I attended a three-day getaway retreat at a spiritual university, in April of 2023.

I grew up in the Christian religion so it shaped my religious worldview. I have been searching for this understanding of the spiritual since moving to New York in 1983 at the age of 22. A lover of reading and developing wisdom, I have read the majority of the Bible, Quran, and parts of the Egyptian Book of the Dead with a hint of Hindu mythology as well.

After all that, I have come to the conclusion that we are all seeking the same divine energy–God–or whatever you identify the divine as. One thing I strongly believe everyone should do is sincerely seek with a pure heart and open mind. When you approach things this way, you will begin to discover that all religions have more in common than they differ.

It is us humans, whose ego gets in the way and thinks our own religious beliefs are the only way to the divine, that causes division and resentment among people. So we manipulate doctrine to achieve our ultimate goals for whatever the reasons or purpose.

This brings me to Reiki.

One of the things that attracted me to Reiki is that it is impossible to manipulate. But, before I knew about this, I was curious about hands-on healing. At church growing up, I heard of healings from the laying of hands but I never witnessed it. How this type of healing worked was never really explained to me nor have I actually ever seen any results from doing it. Reiki is one of many types of hands-on healing so I decided to explore it.

I was having some personal problems and was trying to find a positive solution to deal with them. From there, I was introduced to Eve's Sanctum Salon where the people discussed working with energy and healing. I learned about Reiki from that group.

After being introduced to Reiki and learning in detail how it works, Reiki made a lot of sense to me because it reminded me of how electricity works. Similar to Reiki, you cannot actually see electricity, but you can see the results from its effects. For example, a light bulb glowing or an electric stove element heating up. The reason that I use electricity as a metaphor for Reiki is because like Reiki, electricity flows. It has to have a medium, such as wires or some other means, to travel even though you can't physically see it. Reiki moves in the same way through the body. You can't see it. However, the body feels the effect of it, in the same way that a light bulb glows with the effect of electricity. With Reiki, you may feel pain, relief or relaxation.

With this knowledge, I was still surprised during the 21-day no-meat fast while practicing Reiki exercises, how it gave my body some changes: releasing excessive fluids, toxins, etc. and feeling light and clean internally.

While doing the Reiki hand positions for the twenty-one days, at times, excessive heat in some hand positions were more noticeable than other positions. Somewhere midway in the 21-day exercise I had so much heat generated in particular areas, I thought something was wrong with me! I paused for a bit then continued to the end of the practice that night.

Another thing I observed through the practice happened during my daily meditation. I found it difficult to get rid of the monkey mind. What I mean by monkey mind here is that while you are doing Reiki your mind strays to some other thoughts. My thoughts were always taking over. I would think about something that I did during that day or some other moment in time which has nothing to do with the Reiki. After intentional practice, I found that if I can get rid of the monkey mind and stay in a meditative state, I can achieve great results.

You can actually feel something happening when you get into a meditative state of mind and use Reiki. It's like you are moving a flow of electricity through your body wherever you have your hands. This is when I truly began to understand what is meant by healing of the hands. But, I still doubted whether it truly worked until I noticed a change in my body.

Since I was seventeen years old, I have suffered migraine headaches. After completing my 21-days of Reiki, one difference I noticed is that the severity of my migraines has shifted. Either I need much less medication or they will just be milder when they appear and go away without medication.

Still, I wondered: Is it a coincidence that my headache would go away while performing Reiki or was it working? I decided to test it. On several occasions, when my headache would come I would perform Reiki as I described earlier and observed the same results: my headache would go away. I took that as a confirmation that maybe Reiki truly works. I repeated my experiment over and over again and obtained the same results.

Finally, another interesting result from Reiki has been that I can feel where there's a problem in a part of the body. My experiments with this have been with my wife who suffers foot pain. When I work on her feet, I find myself able to pinpoint the pain spots at times. I enjoy helping others feel better, that's the reason I want to get more experience doing Reiki with others.

It is an honor to share my Reiki experiences with you. Meeting Eve and learning Reiki must have been destiny because I have been reading and searching for the things in life that are beyond the physical that exist spiritually or metaphysically from an early age. Now, on that journey I feel contentment with the direction that I am going.

Anthony's Creating A Sacred Space Practice

All these years, I've always wanted to create a meditation space. I found a private area in my house, and created a prayer room. To do this, where I would be focused on meditation, energy work, and gratitude to the divine, I took a space that felt comfortable to me.

While my space is six by fifteen, if you are interested in creating your own sacred space you can do this in a much smaller area, if that is what is available to you. The space doesn't have to be large. The most important aspect is that it is in an area where there is not a lot of traffic and you will be less likely to be disturbed. If you are divinely sincere in your desire for a meditation space, you will feel the space that is harmonious for you.

In my space I have a bench and carpet. Either I will sit on the bench or floor depending on how I feel when I enter the room. I often meditate. Sometimes I also stretch and move the energy around my body.

I recommend building an altar.

Some of the items you can consider putting on the altar are:
1. Books of faith that resonate with you (I have a Quran and Bible).

2. A cleansing crystal like a ball of Selenite.

3. Statues that you enjoy. I have two Buddha statues because they represent devotion.

4. Anointing oils - find the ones that align with your scriptural beliefs.

5. Incense for religious worship, aromatherapy and meditation.

If you are divinely sincere, in time all things are possible in creating your sacred space.

My name is Anthony Jones. I studied Electrical Engineering Technology at New York City Technical College and worked for the New York City Transit for thirty years as a signal maintainer. This had me maintaining the signaling system for the railroad and I learned to be totally in the present moment and have a deep listening for the movement of energy.

There were times when I was working that a train was coming and would have killed me if I was not fully aware and practicing deep listening. The understanding of how electricity works helped me to understand how Reiki works. Invisible energy that is there but cannot be seen and only evidenced from the results of its effects.

I am now retired and curious about venturing into the unknown by expanding my understanding of the spiritual side of life. This has led me to begin my studies with Reiki and other modalities.

I am a very easy-going and friendly person, always willing to help someone. I am always curious about the unknown and ready to learn something new at all times. Two of my favorite hobbies are gardening (growing food to eat) and building electronic and electrical projects.

Follow Anthony's journey on Instagram at @jones1036.

Chapter 15

A Foundation for Profound Spiritual Practice

Chandra Maharaj, Master Healer / Metaphysician MS. Transpersonal Psychology Spiritual Counselor

Hello, I'm Chandra Maharaj, a Heart-Centered Master Energy Healer, Medium, Spiritual Counselor, and Therapist.

My focus lies in harmonizing the subtle energy centers within the meridians, chakras, and the auric field to clear blocks and bring about balance within the mind, body, and spirit. Additionally, I serve as an Intuitive Medium, channeling direct and personal messages from elevated consciousness for each client.

You might wonder what propelled me onto this path. In 2009, my trajectory shifted from a career as a Technical Trainer, when our department was reorganized. My supervisor asked me to remain and shift into another department. My body and soul told me "no." A hardcore "no." The company gave me a severance package. I now had the time and no idea what I was supposed to do. I knew that my previous work was not resonating with my purpose. But, I didn't even know my purpose. I just knew that this wasn't right for me.

Fast forward a decade and several career trials later in event and wedding planning, invitation design, retail and volunteer teaching with refugees–I didn't feel fulfilled. There was something missing and I kept getting blocked from going further in my business or career. What I didn't know at the time is that *all along I was getting nudges*. At one point, the nudges became so much that I could no longer ignore them.

The death of a young friend propelled me to ask: "Can this happen to me?" At the time I was fat and stressed to the point of giving myself heart palpitations. After getting a clear bill of health from a heart specialist, I decided to get on a plan to help with my stress. Walking in the park, mediating, and eating more plant-based food.

This in turn led me to a realization that I needed to take care of myself. The nudges of life continued with more deaths and other trials that I couldn't undo or see. Some of these nudges occurred as prompts that I heard inside of me. I didn't always understand or pay attention to them but I realized that there were too many occurrences of death. When my aunt was dying, I heard inside of me: "You need to go" to Texas.

At first I didn't know why I was going to support my mother as she was caring for her sister-in-law as a way of supporting my cousins who were caring for their terminally ill and dying mother. What I did know was that I had to follow my inner voice. My role as caretaker to my cousins became clear once I arrived and helped them get groceries and cooked meals for them, as they spent long hours at the hospital.

"Take a leap," the words came to me at the hospital, followed by, "Be brave." I'm hearing things now and I'm scared. The words indicated that I was supposed to take some kind of action but I didn't know what that might be at the time. Something inside of me was changing. I answered the call in my heart, knowing that my world was about to transform!

The nudges kept coming. One night as I was sitting on the computer finishing up some design work, I kept hearing "energy" over and over again.

What does "energy" mean, I wondered?

What kind of "energy" are we talking about?

Researching online, I stumbled upon the world of "Energy Healing" and discovered the concept of Reiki, a Japanese practice harnessing universal life force energy for holistic healing. Intrigued, I delved deeper, enrolling in alternative healing courses, including a transformative program at Kennesaw University.

My journey continued as I pursued in-person Reiki training. At the attunement I was radiating heat! Many different things were happening in my body. This training helped me recognize the movement of energy in my body. What it felt like and how I perceived it. Feeling all kinds of things in my body, I wondered: "What am I supposed to do with this?" I even remember on my drive home as I reached for my water, I felt the resonating energy of my cup. Wow! My mind was blown. I wanted to know more.

"There's more," my inner voice told me in such a way that I understood this was a really strong call. Reiki was the first step on the journey. And yet, every path I tried to take for further studies, Pranic Healing, or other courses, weren't working out for me. It was a dead end.

Out of the blue, Delphi Spiritual University popped up on my computer. When I called them to inquire, the man who answered was like: "There's a requirement for the metaphysical certification program. There's a class at the end of July to fulfill this requirement.

We'll let you know if we have space." I knew that I would be in that course.

At the end of the week he called back to say: "We have a drop out. You can come." Like Texas, and other experiences that had been happening to me over the course of the past few years, I didn't know what I was walking into. I held faith that these nudges were leading me in the right direction. I began my studies at Delphi.

Through rigorous study and introspection, I evolved into a multifaceted practitioner, delving into the realms of Spiritual Psychology, Mediumship, and Crystal Healing.

Reiki served as my gateway to profound self-discovery, propelling me towards inner child and shadow work, enriching my understanding of self and others.

Presently, I am dedicated to cultivating my practice, offering an array of healing modalities both at Centre Spring MD and at my private space, while aspiring to advance my studies as an Energy Doctor, specializing in Energy Medicine and Spiritual Anatomy.

My ultimate vision encompasses establishing a holistic healing sanctuary, embracing individuals from diverse paths seeking complementary practices to conventional medicine.

Chandra's Checking in with Self Practice

All along we are getting nudges. At one point, the nudges will become so much that you can no longer ignore them. If we shut them down something bigger comes to shake us.

If we go inside to ask about the nudges then they keep coming. This practice can help you to identify the nudges and learn what they are trying to tell you.

Also, it will help you with recognizing and releasing the fear that may arise as you listen to the inner voice of your higher self.

1. Lie down comfortably in a space that feels safe and secure. If you would like to close your eyes, feel free to do so.

2. Take a few full deep breaths in through your nose, pulling the breath in until the stomach expands. Then a full breath out, bringing the body into a state of full relaxation.

3. Sense or feel where in the body is calling your attention. Is there a pain, feeling of unease, sensations: tingling twitch whatever it may be?

4. When you have located the sensation ask: What do I need at this time? Listen or feel for the answer. Let whatever comes into your awareness come into your awareness. Acknowledge the pain, emotion, vision or whatever sensation without trying to change it.

5. Thank these parts for showing you what it has shown you.

6. Believing, or not, in the intention is all that is necessary to heal. Ask for healing to come to the area, sensation, emotion, or whatever.

7. Know and feel that the healing has come.

8. Take another deep breath to come back into the present. Begin to wiggle the fingers and toes. Say "thank you" and then open your eyes.

Chandra is a Medium, Master Healer and Spiritual Counselor in the areas of Energy, Sound and Crystal Healing. She works with the chakras to help clear blockages and bring about a balance in the mind, body, and spirit. Chandra is also an Intuitive Medium that channels a higher state of consciousness to tap into messages from Spirit. She also specializes in Spiritual Therapy working with trauma patterns in the Child Self and how it shows up in your adult life.

Chandra was always very sensitive to energies from a young age but in 2018, she experienced a spiritual awakening caused by some major life-changing events. This catapulted her into studying and working with energies to further fine-tune her gifts.

She plans to continue her studies in Energy Medicine which shows how imbalances in our meridians, chakras and auric field affect our physical, emotional, and spiritual well-being causing "Dis-ease" in our bodies.

Connect with Chandra @Chandra_Energy_Medicine on Instagram or email chandra.energy.medicine@gmail.com.

Chapter 16

White-Knuckled with Anxiety

Eve Smith, MA, Reiki Master Trainer, Gong Master Practitioner, RYT 200

"I can't do this," I muttered to the ceiling, heart racing. A cold sweat gathered on my brow as I realized, *I **have** to do this*. The sun crept across the room, marking the hours I lay there, struggling to take a deep breath. I still had an hour and a half before I needed to be at the ferry terminal to board for Macau.

"I can't do this." My voice trembled as I reached for my phone, torn between sending a text or forcing myself to get up and go. My friends, who I hadn't seen in years, had organized a beautiful trip to Macau. As much as it terrified me, I had to go. If I didn't, my anxiety would win.

I opened my friend's contact and started typing.

> So sorry, something has come up and I don't feel well. Can't make it.

The message offered temporary relief, and I closed my phone. Taking a deep breath, I thought, "I can do this." I showered, imagining the fear and anxiety washing down the drain. Then, stepping outside into the Hong Kong heat, my heart raced again. Putting one foot in front of the other, I navigated to the MTR, Hong Kong's underground train system. On the surface, no one knew the battle I was fighting. My white-knuckled grip on the escalator was the only outward sign. I took a deep breath and boarded the train. The doors slid shut behind me, committing me to moving forward.

As the train pulled away, I deleted the apology text. Today, I'd beaten my anxiety.

But tomorrow?

Tomorrow was another battle.

Simple tasks—like taking the train or boarding the ferry—became monumental with anxiety. Leaving my room felt like climbing Everest. I spent hours trying to calm my nerves, while my life was swallowed by fear. My resilience had crumbled, and anxiety held the reins.

I hadn't always struggled with anxiety. But after living through a war zone, a revolution, and a natural disaster, anxiety began to consume me. What were once simple tasks now felt impossible, and my days were filled with more apology texts than not. Yet, Hong Kong, with its stability and dramatic landscapes, had become my healing ground. Successfully boarding the ferry to Macau felt like a small victory—proof that Hong Kong was helping me regain control of my life.

In addition to taking Reiki with Stephen Clasper at the Shakti Healing Centre, I also worked with a trusted therapist. I knew the journey back to health would take time. I had to push back against my perfectionist tendencies and expectations for rapid results, giving myself the time and space I needed to heal.

At my lowest point, I found myself unable to do normal activities with friends. Even at work, I had extreme reactions to things that shouldn't have evoked such large responses. A simple work email would send me spiraling into panic, heart racing as if the email was a harbinger of disaster. Often, I imagined worst-case scenarios, feeling overwhelmed before I even opened the message. More often than not, the emails were innocuous. But my body was convinced that each one meant something dreadful.

This wasn't sustainable. I couldn't avoid emails, and I couldn't keep reacting this way.

Before I started my Reiki re-training, my therapist taught me an exercise called box breathing. Every inhale and exhale formed the sides of a box in my mind. With each breath, the box grew larger, expanding as I slowly calmed my stress response. The simplicity of the exercise helped me focus, allowing my mind to be occupied by something other than anxiety.

Meditation was also part of my practice. I struggled with it at first—my mind ran a mile a minute. But I committed to five minutes of box breathing, followed by short sessions of meditation, slowly increasing the time I could sit in quiet concentration. Over weeks, I went from fifteen seconds of meditation to a minute, then beyond.

My Reiki Level 1 retraining was the perfect complement to the other practices I was developing. Stephen emphasized mindset and reframing to shift energy. This helped me deepen my understanding of how my thoughts shaped my emotions and experiences.

As I worked through my 21-day self-Reiki practice, I began to feel more balanced. My hands would get hot in a certain way during the practice, for example, when placed on my head which is a sign of the high anxiety and stress I had been carrying. I knew this because they would get hot in another way when placed on an injury. But as the days went on, the heat in my head faded, replaced by a soothing, soft energy. My stress reactions diminished, and my meditation practice expanded to fifteen minutes.

I could also feel a shift in my daily life. The terror that used to grip me at the thought of leaving my room started to ease. Instead of dreading social interactions, I looked forward to them. Reiki had begun reconnecting my mind and body, bringing me back to myself.

Reiki, paired with breathwork, meditation, and therapy, helped me regain control over my life. It became foundational to my healing, especially when I added yoga and sound healing into the mix. Together, these practices transformed my relationship with anxiety and brought me back into balance.

If you're experiencing any of the symptoms I've described, picking up this book is one of the many steps that will take you to where you would prefer to be. Healing doesn't happen overnight. Box breathing, meditation, and Reiki can all be done anywhere, at any time, offering tools for relief and balance. With Reiki Level 1, you focus on yourself and bringing your mind and body into harmony. This process has been profoundly transformative in my life.

We all start somewhere, and it's important to honor your journey, wherever you may be. For me, the commitment to Reiki self-practice, day in and day out, helped me understand the intimate connection between my mind and body. Through this process, I found peace, balance, and eventually, an expansion of my abilities. Just as Chandra mentioned in her story, I, too, found my psychic gifts evolving as I continued my healing journey.

If you need immediate emotional support, reach out to 988 Lifeline in the US.

Eve's Practices

Box Breathing

Mentioned in my story, I used box breathing to help calm and ground me.

Here's how to do it:

- Bring yourself to a comfortable position whether it is seated or lying down. Allow your eyes to close or your gaze to become unfocused.

- Take a moment to listen to your breath. Observe it without trying to change it. Notice the sound of your inhale and exhale. Notice the speed or pace of your inhale and exhale. Notice the temperature of your breath as it comes in and goes out.

- As you breathe in, imagine building a box. See one side, construct the other side, and the other sides until you are complete. As you exhale, construct a box around the first box that is slightly bigger.

- With every breath build a slightly bigger box. Trying to build the box as big as possible.

- Stop when it feels right for you.

- Journal what you notice about your practice. This does not have to be long. Some of the notes I take are: noting the moon phase, whether or not I can concentrate, and any interesting thoughts that pop up.

Walking and Seated Meditation Practices

I offer you two different versions of meditation. The first is a walking meditation with a focus on using breath and movement to bring the mind into a state of deep relaxation. Walking meditations allow the mind to relax and may also be used to receive insights from your higher self. You might also receive answers to questions that you have whether they are ordinary questions: relationships, work, large purchases, among others. Or, if you are looking for creative problem solving. This practice develops your connection to your intuition.

The second is a seated meditation that builds an awareness of and a connection to the world around you through sound. The sounds of nature can be both activating and healing depending on your mindset and past experiences. The purpose of this meditation is to observe your responses rather than engage with them. When you see your responses, you have information about yourself that is useful.

Slowing down and listening in nature also allows you to connect with the natural cycles and rhythms of the world. This releases tension and stress. This meditation connects you to each of the sounds that make up the sonic landscape of the area you are observing. Within this landscape you can move your consciousness outward to observe sound that occurs in the distance. You can also focus your consciousness on the body, moving it to observe your own life force energy—the heart. Both practices deeply impact the mind-body connection and create a sense of ease and harmony.

After each practice is an invitation to journal. Taking notes about what happened, how you felt, what you experienced, and what you would like to keep or change about each experience helps you to fine tune your meditation to something that feels fulfilling and fully yours.

Here is my **walking meditation practice** (adapt as you please):

- Walk into the woods. Either continue to walk and adapt the walk to your breath or find a safe area to sit.

- Forest Bathing is a recognized healthy living activity in Japan called "Shinrinyoku." This involves going into the forest to breathe in the natural chemical releases of trees. When absorbed by the body, these chemicals stimulate the immune system and have been found to reduce anxiety, stress, depression, and anger (Li, 2010). Forest Bathing takes only a few minutes and can immediately lighten your mood.

- If you wish to continue walking, pause and take a moment to thank the forest, offering appreciation for its presence. Take a few deep breaths. These purposeful acts will shift your consciousness, slowing you down.

- **Set an intention for your practice.**

- Then, as you walk, focus on feeling each part of the foot as it touches the ground from heel to the toes. Walking with this awareness if you would like to time yourself to your breath, you might inhale step forward and exhale and shift your weight in preparation to step forward. Or, you might step pause, breathe in and out, step again. There are many variations. Use what feels best in your body.

- When you are preparing to finish your walk, pause to take a few deep breaths and thank the forest.

- Journal about your experience: How did this meditation feel in your body and mind? Any thoughts that arose while you were walking? What did you like? What would you do differently next time (maybe choosing different words or visualizations)? What question do you still have that you might find answers to online?

Here is my **seated meditation practice:**

- If you decide to sit, take a moment to look around you observing the forest. At this point, I also look up to make certain I'm not seated under a branch or tree that might fall.

- Take a few deep breaths.

- Set an intention. Continue to breathe deeply.

- Close your eyes or allow them to become unfocused on the ground in front of you and focus on your hearing. What is the symphony of sounds you can hear in the forest? How does it sound as a whole?

- Now, focus on individual sounds. What is the furthest sound you can hear? Can you identify what makes that sound? What are the other sounds that are far away? Try to notice as many sounds as possible. Whether or not you can identify them does not matter as much as spending time with those sounds. Listen to their frequency, tone, and how they make you feel. Do they evoke physical responses? Do they evoke emotional responses?

- Begin to bring your listening closer to yourself. What are the sounds you hear within your immediate area (within ten feet)? Within five feet? Immediately around you?

- Bring your listening to your body. Observe the sound of your breath. What other sounds do you hear? Observe the sound of your heart. Focus on the sound of your heart. If it feels good, while you focus on the heartbeat you might place one hand over the heart and the other over the diaphragm. Spend a few minutes here.

- If it feels right to you, imagine a beautiful, loving white light from the universe coming into your body from the crown of your head. See this light begin to pulse with the rhythm of your heart. Using your inhale, imagine this light spreading throughout your body. On the exhale, release any tense energy the light has displaced from your body. Continue to inhale and spread the light around your body until you believe it to be filling every cell. Stay in this elevated vibration for a few moments.

- Allow your listening to expand from yourself out to your immediate area.

- Then, when you are ready, take a moment to journal what you noticed about how you felt in the meditation. How did you feel physically? Did you notice any changes in your body (shoulders loosening, stomach not as tense)? Emotionally? You might also like to look at how successful you felt in completing the meditation. What did you like? What would you do differently next time (maybe choosing different words or visualizations)? What questions do you still have that you might find answers to online?

Sound and Reiki practitioner Eve Smith is a lifelong learner whose journey has taken her through teaching roles and ultimately into the world of holistic healing practices. For over fifteen years, Eve worked with the English Language Programs of the US. State Department and also lectured at universities around the world.

In 2013, after a profound experience in Bali, Eve learned Reiki. She continues to build her Reiki capacity by studying with multiple teachers. Reiki was foundational to her creating a deep connection with her higher self. The work continues through shamanic work, yoga, meditation, and sound. This connection to the higher self provides an *inner sanctum* which is available to all and offers a safe, loving *internal* anchor through difficult times.

Eve is passionate about sharing her journey and helping others discover their own paths to balance and joy through transformative practices. Whether it's finding inner peace or managing stress, Eve is dedicated to helping clients tailor these modalities to fit their unique needs and create a fulfilling and harmonious life.

You can connect with Eve at www.sanctumwithevesmyth.comfor events, Reiki classes or private sessions, or join the journey at https://evesmyth.substack.com/for access to the inner workings of a Reiki, sound, and shamanic practitioner.

Chapter 17

Healing Animals with Reiki

Felicia Holden, Reiki Master, Therapeutic Sound Practitioner, Certified in EFT/Meridian Tapping

While a student at Indiana University in Bloomington Indiana, my Reiki journey began. I studied Reiki Level I and II from a Reiki master I met through the community named Donald J. Burns. At that time, I was interested in learning Reiki to help animals because I had become heavily involved in animal rescue and also had received my wildlife rehabilitation license. Working with the animals and classes kept me busy. And I never knew when I was going to encounter an animal in need.

There was one time, sparrows had built nests in the lighting fixtures at a bank downtown. The bank was replacing the lights and put around twenty-five sparrow nests on the sidewalk. My building was beside the bank and I was on my way home when I saw the frantic parents crying out and trying to get their babies out of the light fixtures that were about to go to the dump. It took me over an hour but I successfully pulled all the babies out to save them. There were fifteen baby birds in various stages of development. I gave Reiki to all of them but they were so small, some of them didn't even have feathers. I took care of them, feeding them by hand several times a day and offering them Reiki and love. It seemed to help them, however, I sadly lost several. Thankfully the remaining three babies flew to freedom after a few weeks.

I also found Reiki very helpful for calming sick and abused animals that I personally rescued or worked with at the local shelter. After sharing Reiki, I observed that the animals trusted me quicker and healed faster from any injuries. Over the next decade or so, I focused my Reiki practice on animals and sometimes human friends, too.

Jumping to 2016, I started volunteering with children and horses at Stride Ahead, which is an equine assisted therapy program in Decatur, Georgia. Stride Ahead was established to assist veterans and children with disabilities. While we groomed and prepared the horses for the therapy ride, I would intuitively share Reiki with the horses to calm them and to help focus them on providing a successful session. Other volunteers would notice how calm the horses would become during Reiki and afterwards.

One of the horses, Justin, would get excited when I came out to the barn. He would sometimes run out to the gate to meet me, which is not usual behavior for some of the horses at that barn. One time when Justin was sick he refused food. I gave him Reiki and rubbed some essential oils on my hands and let him sniff the oils. It appeared that he was having nausea and the oil helped to settle his tummy. Immediately after the Reiki session I offered him food out of my hand and he ate it. Similar experiences occurred with my sick pets Kudzu and Stanley. Animals respond beautifully to Reiki.

The trained support horses were not the only ones in need of Reiki at the barn. There was a retired racehorse who also lived there. Before arriving at the barn, he had been severely abused by his previous owners, causing him to charge or nip at most people who got close to him.

After observing this behavior for a while, I wondered if Reiki might help him relax and trust more. I approached his rider and asked if I could share Reiki with him. She thought it was worth a try. Within a few moments, I saw the terror and anger in his eyes begin to subside as he relaxed and enjoyed the Reiki treatment. His rider was surprised at the horse's positive behavior during and after a session and that Justin had allowed me to lightly touch him without nipping me.

During the pandemic, I attended Reiki shares and other classes led by Reiki Master Eve Smith. This renewed my passion for Reiki on people because I witnessed the positive outcome others were experiencing. Clients have said it helps with their anxiety, depression, self-healing, and sleep. I've also witnessed Reiki helping clients resolve emotional issues and triggers. Wanting to give more, I studied at the Master level from a Tibetan Buddhist monk named Tenzin Lama in 2022. This was one of the biggest turning points on my path to healing and my desire to share what I have learned with others.

Because of the positive outcomes I've witnessed and for professional development, I continue to learn as much as I can regarding spiritual healing and continue to take classes in person and online. Every day I am grateful for the opportunity to share Reiki.

I offer Reiki to people at Decatur Healing Arts as well as other locations around Atlanta. Additionally, my passion continues for sharing Reiki with animals and I am available for animal Reiki sessions.

Felicia's Grounding Practice

It is important to establish a regular practice of grounding to help you focus on your path. This can be accomplished by spending time in nature and perhaps finding a quiet space outside to meditate and practice conscious breathing.

Try the following:

- Lie down directly upon the ground and begin to focus on your breath.

- After a few minutes of breath focus, do a full-body stretch by extending your arms above your head and stretching out your legs.

- Then, begin a full body scan by starting at your head and working your way to your toes and noticing the places in your body where you feel any tension or discomfort.

- Bring your attention to those areas of tension and discomfort and consciously breathe into them while imagining discomfort flowing into the earth where the energy will be used to nurture something else.

- As you feel ready to wrap up, remind yourself of one thing you are truly grateful for. If you feel compelled to do so, this would be a good time to journal.

A Reiki Self-Care Practice

I wanted to invite those readers who are already Reiki certified to try a Reiki and sound practice.

As a suggestion, my daily self-care practice includes a morning meditation and self-Reiki while playing music such as meditation music or Solfeggio Frequencies. Solfeggio frequencies are believed to profoundly affect the conscious and subconscious mind in order to stimulate healing and to promote well-being.

After meditation, I reflect on and journal about:

- what I'm grateful for,

- what I want to focus on in my life,

- I also create a list of achievements that I'm proud of.

This reminds me of my successes and that I'm strong and capable of achieving my dreams.

Felicia is a certified Usui Reiki Master Practitioner. She received her Reiki Master training in 2022 from a Tibetan Buddhist monk named Tenzin Lama and, while in college, received her Reiki Level I & II Certification from Donald J. Burns. She also took Reiki continuing education courses with Reiki Master Eve Smith. Felicia holds additional certifications in teaching meditation, Emotional Freedom Technique (meridian tapping), and Crystal Bowl Sound Therapy.

During a session with Felicia, you will feel relaxed and rejuvenated. With compassion and intuition she focuses on the areas in need of support; balances and clears the chakras; helps to release any negative or blocked energy; and guides you along your journey to self-healing. She has witnessed many positive changes in others by sharing the nurturing and healing practice of Reiki.

Felicia believes that Reiki is meant for everyone, including animals and she has shared Reiki with horses, dogs, and cats. She volunteers with children and horses at Stride Ahead, which is an equine assisted therapy program.

Felicia would be honored to be a part of your healing journey. You can reach her at Felicia.holden1@gmail.com.

Chapter 18

Outta Control Solar Plexus, I Need the Keys to My Lexus

Shaneka Hunter, CMA, AS, BS loading

Several months after being shown the daily practice of Reiki by the beautiful Eve Smith, I found myself, the day after Christmas, experiencing the absolute worst back pain shooting from the lower right sacral region and radiating across my back before settling into a throbbing.

This pain was a twenty-eight on a pain scale of 0-10! For almost three weeks, I hobbled, limped and whined about this pain. The simple things such as using the restroom, cooking, lying down, getting in and out of the car easily drew tears from my eyes. I tried:

- the chiropractor

- multiple rounds of steroids

- pain meds

- NSAIDS

- steroid injections

- rotating heat and ice packs

- using extra pillows

- stretching

- even massage therapy.

When I say not a single thing worked...NOT A SINGLE THING WORKED!!!

So, I reached out to my lovely Reiki teacher and she politely asked, "So, have you tried performing Reiki on yourself since the pain began?"

With the most profound feeling of humility, I slowly replied "Umm, no ma'am" as I shook and hung my head studiously in self-disappointment.

That same night of our conversation, I hopped into action and performed the 21-day self Reiki practice I learned from my traditional Usui Reiki course, on myself. Beginning with a light 10-minute meditation, listening to wordless music to calm my mind, I naturally flowed into a state where my mind and body met peacefully.

With my eyes closed, I began my Reiki self-session. Slowly working my hand placements over the appropriate chakras in their respectful order, by the time I reached my solar plexus, I began to feel lighter, more open, less tense, less defeated emotionally and physically.

I could feel the inflammation easing in my joints, the pain I had felt for weeks was beginning to let go of me, and I was letting go of it.

Listen my dear reader, I am a firm believer that we all possess the Universal Gift of the power to bring healing to oneself and to others. With an open mind, I ask you to believe me when I say after only one session of head to toe Reiki on myself, I instantly began to not only feel the most heartwarming and sensory relieving ease in my agonizing back pain, but I also experienced the frequency of self-love that radiated throughout my body.

My perception of my pain shifted and I was able to see and consider that maybe the sudden back pain was trapped Kundalini energy and possibly unresolved emotions that needed my attention. That needed my love, concern and awareness.

When I caught up with Eve again to update her about my experience, she lovingly chuckled as I told her that I was feeling much better. That I could walk, stretch without tears, sleep again and even dance!! Yes, dance. I had forgotten just how much I loved to dance, even just around my house to my favorite music, until I literally could not, ooh child!!!

Reiki has helped me look at pain in my body so much differently now. I understand that not all pain, although experienced in the physical, comes from the body. Discomfort in our physical bodies, can originate in our thoughts, and in our minds as trapped energy needing to be felt, understood, accepted and lovingly released.

What I learned and what I would invite you to do, dear reader, is to always consider the origin of pain when you feel it. When you understand the possible underlying causes, you can, like I did, find the meaning and how best to remedy it.

Shaneka's Clearing Practice

Next time your body decides to communicate via pain or discomfort in the physical body, ask:

- Has this pain ever happened before? What was going on at that time?

- What is your body trying to communicate to you?

- Is the discomfort related to emotions or physical movement?

- Is the area of discomfort near a chakra (see the list below)? If so, which one?

- Is there a correlation between that chakra and the emotional body?

- Behaviors can create emotional responses in the body, i.e. negative self-talk may cause overeating and feelings of defeat. What emotions or behaviors can you give more attention to that may alleviate the discomfort with grace and love?

Chakra Guide

Here is my perception of the chakras and their emotional correlation. Use this as a soft guide if it resonates with you.

Seven Main Chakras and Their Unpleasant Emotional Influences

    1. Crown: Not being in alignment with your higher self.

    2. Third eye (forehead): Lack of focus and creativity

    3. Throat: Fear to speak authentically

    4. Heart: Lack of self-empathy

    5. Solar Plexus (stomach area): Not feeling in control; powerlessness; negative self-image

    6. Sacral (just under the belly button): Fear of intimacy; codependency; feelings of unworthiness

    7. Root (bottom of torso): Too much yang (masculine) energy; fight or flight; ruminating;

    8. This isn't a chakra but please consider, E-G-O.

Take a deep breath and be gentle with yourself here as you ask: How can this chakra information be useful? How can I integrate this nugget of wisdom into my daily practice?

Self-awareness is a life-long process. Rome wasn't built in one day, so take it one step at a time.

Finally, discomfort in our physical bodies, can manifest from our thoughts, unresolved stress, trauma, even negative self-talk in our minds that has become trapped energy that is needing to be felt in its

entirety, fully understood, gracefully accepted and then lovingly released. I am forever grateful to know the power of healing and self-love
through Reiki.

Shaneka's words of wisdom.

I'm ruminating - my root's cutting up!

My crown's feeling down - pick your head up!

I want off the boat - say it from your throat!

Shaneka Hunter is a powerhouse of love and light. She serves her community with a really big heart, grace, compassion, and a desire to understand other people's journeys. Through sharing her own journey, Shaneka, hopes to assist others in their healing as she continues to heal herself.

Although Shaneka's path started out murky, as a survivor of childhood and adult sexual abuse, she is committed to transmuting her suffering into love and nourishment for herself and others. Shaneka believes that everybody has a story and the medicine is in how we tell it.

Connect with Shaneka via Instagram: _naturally_nikki333

Chapter 19

Connecting to My Inner Passion

Susanne McMurry, Reiki Master
Practitioner, Certified Yoga Nidra
Instructor, RYT 200

> "Smile, Breathe, and Go
> Slowly." Thich Nhat
> Hanh

These five words have been my mantra for many years.

For most of my adult life I have searched for a line of work that aligned with my passion for helping others. Despite exploring various job opportunities where I could make a difference, I consistently felt unfulfilled at the end of each workday. It became increasingly clear to me that while our professions don't define us entirely, finding genuine joy and satisfaction in how we spend the majority of our waking hours is important.

Looking back I now realize my misunderstanding of what my purpose was, meant that I spent the majority of my time in workspaces or situations that depleted my energy. There were evenings where I worked until late into the night to meet the c-suite's deadline, crying over cold pizza at my desk. For years I was pulled into situations where I may have perceived myself as "helping people" but not in the way that left me feeling joyful. Only beginning to understand what brought me joy outside of work could bring me joy at work, I was searching for how to use my time without any real knowledge on how to find that. It wasn't until much later that I learned about the true power of tapping into, and listening to, my intuition and my body.

In 2010 I began experiencing a lot of anxiety. It seemed to come out of nowhere, my chest was heavy and I felt like I couldn't take a deep breath. I felt dizzy and afraid I was going to faint when I was in large crowds of people at a concert, or even in a busy grocery store. (Little did I know at the time that I was unknowingly taking on other people's energy.) I met with a therapist who said that I wasn't breathing properly. My breath was shallow and I wasn't breathing into my stomach. She taught me a few tricks to "snap out of it" when I was hit with anxiety, and she suggested that I try gentle yoga classes. I'm so grateful for that appointment, it set me on my current path!

During my first yoga class I felt a huge release, like a "pop" and a few tears ran down my face. That was the beginning of re-discovering harmony in my mind and body. Yoga taught me the power of breath and balance through movement and meditation. It also introduced me to the chakras or energy centers in my body.

It wasn't until 2016 after my father passed away that I first experienced the powerful healing that comes from universal life force energy, Reiki. (Rei) being universal life force, (Ki) being energy. At that time I was holding a lot of stress and grief and tried multiple modalities to help relieve the pressure I was feeling in my body and mind. My first Reiki session was a transformational experience. Although I had no idea what Reiki was or how it worked, I was open to trying it. As the practitioner's hands gently rested over my heart, a flood of tears cascaded down my cheeks, releasing layers of accumulated stress. It felt as though a weight had been lifted from my chest, allowing me to breathe deeply once more. From that moment on, I was captivated. I sought out yoga classes and events that incorporated Reiki, the two practices together were very calming for my nervous system. I attended group sessions and private sessions and just continued to peel away layers of negative energy and stress. I couldn't explain how it was working at that time, but I didn't feel like I needed to. I began to trust my intuition and really notice how I was feeling: lighter, gentler towards myself and others.

Fast forward to 2021 during the COVID pandemic. Seeing the need in Atlanta for the unhoused, underprivileged, mental health, etc., it fractured me. Even more disconnected and frustrated in my corporate job, I decided to leave. I wanted to be a part of amazing organizations and people out there serving others. Knowing I needed to get more involved in my community and find my own authentic way to be of service, I spent almost a year seeking out different volunteer opportunities. I met so many beautiful humans along the way.

Simultaneously, I decided to enroll in a 200-hour yoga teacher training to deepen my own practice and to continue learning and growing. Towards the end of the year I accepted a new position at Advanced Wellness of Atlanta. Their mission aligned with where I was at that point in my life and it was another experience to learn and grow. However, I still felt like something was missing, there was something more for me to do. Needing guidance, I began searching for workshops and happened upon a heart opening workshop led by Chandra Maharaj. It was a beautiful class with meditation and journaling, and at some point during my meditation my subconscious mind encouraged me to explore learning Reiki. I enrolled in Reiki

Level 1 with Eve Smith immediately and dedicated myself to learning and practicing.

I'm now a Reiki Master practitioner and I absolutely love this work! Reiki has changed my life, and allowed me, in turn, to facilitate safe and supportive sessions for others, giving clients the space to bring their body into harmony, work through difficult situations, or just feel more balanced.

Reiki has deepened my self-confidence. For example, I have always had a fear of public speaking (yet another reason I had no desire to teach yoga) but once I was attuned to the energy I felt a connection between my mind and my physical body. Additionally, I felt more of a connection to my higher self, source, and pure love. And I also started to realize I had to open myself up, be vulnerable, so I could share my story in a meaningful way.

As I practiced and grew as a teacher, opportunities to teach yoga and become more involved in the local community continued popping up. Wanting to expand my practice, I traveled to Yogi Hari's Ashram in Florida and attended a Yoga Nidra training with Chitra Sukhu. It was another life-changing experience, opening my eyes to even more ways that we move energy, release blockages, and release stress. Yoga Nidra and Reiki gave me faith that we all have the capacity to bring in so much light into our lives, even during times of hardship.

My mission to provide people with the support needed to achieve wellness and balance in their lives through Reiki, Yoga Nidra and Restorative Yoga & Meditation led me to start my wellness company, Serenity Healing Arts, LLC in 2022. This is beyond anything I would have expected in my life given that I hated presenting myself to others. The practices gave me an inner confidence and knowing that I can do all things. From this openness, I collaborate with wellness colleagues and local nonprofits, like Compassionate Atlanta, that offer free or discounted wellness services by organizing events that bring awareness to the needs of the Atlanta community.

My life has completely transformed over the past seven years. I've come a long way since feeling disconnected in the corporate work world and having panic attacks at concerts and on public transportation. The lifestyle enhancements that Reiki, yoga, and Yoga Nidra unfolded in and through me continues to inspire me to develop compassion and resilience towards myself and others. This is the core of my offerings.

Susanne's Practice

It's extremely important to have self practice. Without dedication to your own practice and energy, it is easy to lose yourself. (In this work especially.) You may have noticed that when you are in a crowded space, you take on emotions or feelings that don't feel like yours. Like you are totally fine and then you are suddenly pissed off or want to cry. This is an indication that you are possibly feeling someone else's energy. I'd like to teach you a quick practice to come back into your own energy.

One simple way to ground is to place your feet on the earth and imagine your beautiful strong roots growing down into the earth, through every layer until they reach the center. Place one hand on the heart and one hand on the belly as you do this. Take in a few deep nourishing breaths, bringing the air all the way to the stomach. As you exhale, feel your body relax. Each breath deepens your connection to the earth and strengthens your energetic roots. What I love about this practice is that it can be done anytime, anywhere.

Note: Reiki is a beautiful complement to allopathic medicine and other forms of complementary medicine. If you are interested in learning Reiki, I invite you to find a teacher who will continue to offer guidance and opportunities to learn and grow. There are many teachers throughout the world who are in line with this idea.

When I researched who I wished to study with I looked for: Reiki Practice offerings, continuing education, and activity in the community. This is your opportunity to explore this incredible energy, choosing the right teacher will make a huge difference on how to move forward and what direction you go with it.

Susanne discovered yoga and the power of breath in 2010. Her teaching journey began with a RYT 200 certification in 2021. Studying under Chitra Sukhu, for her Yoga Nidra certification, Susanne's heart-centered approach to teaching revolves around the belief that true well-being emerges not only from personal practice but from the collective energy we create together. Focused on restorative practices, she is dedicated to offering classes that provide a sanctuary for your nervous system.

After her father passed away in 2016, Susanne explored Reiki as a way to deal with the grief. Her first Reiki session that year changed her life, leading her on a path of healing and growth that continues today. In 2022, she became a Reiki practitioner knowing it would alter the trajectory of her life. She received her certifications up to Usui Reiki Master Practitioner under Eve Smith.

Each class or session with Susanne is an invitation to explore the innate wisdom of the body, calm the nervous system, and connect with the collective energy that surrounds us. All are welcome.

I would love to hear from you if you are interested in working with me or collaborating on a wellness project! graceandshanti@gmail.com, graceandshanti.wixsite.com, or IG @serenity.healing.artsatl

Chapter 20

Conclusion: The Benefits of Reiki

Alice shared how Reiki helped her heal neuropathy and a heart murmur, while also teaching her to slow down and offer Reiki to the earth and her garden. Through these practices, she feels more peaceful, relaxed, and protected.

Anthony discovered that Reiki moves through the body like electricity, aiding his detox process by releasing excess fluids and toxins, leaving him feeling light and clean internally. Reiki also calmed his mind during meditation and significantly improved his migraines.

Chandra revealed that Reiki is a foundational practice that taught her to trust her higher self, ultimately leading her to become a Heart-Centered Master Energy Healer.

Eve described how Reiki taught her to trust in the unseen and in the natural world. It brought her a sense of community and healing from paralyzing anxiety attacks.

Felicia demonstrated how offering Reiki to animals can help with their nausea, pain, and anxiety.

Shaneka's experience showed how her pain journey shifted from extreme discomfort to no pain at all, thanks to Reiki.

Susanne shared how Reiki bridged the gap between the draining corporate world, where she thought she was supposed to be, and her true calling to help others. Reiki also eased her fear of public speaking and led her to a deep, fulfilling practice of Yoga Nidra.

These stories offer just a glimpse into how Reiki has touched the lives of individuals. You may be wondering, "What can Reiki do for me?" Reiki's benefits are diverse and deeply personal. While each experience is unique, common themes include stress reduction, emotional healing, physical relief, and spiritual connection.

However, it is important to remember that Reiki communicates with each of us in different ways. While the symbols and experiences discussed may hold common meanings, your spirit may guide you to a different understanding. Always listen to your heart and intuition, as they will reveal the personal significance of each encounter.

Chapter 21
Finding A Reiki Teacher

Guidance by Susanne & Eve

Susanne writes, Reiki is a beautiful complement to allopathic medicine and other forms of complementary medicine. If you are interested in learning Reiki, I invite you to find a teacher who will continue to offer guidance and opportunities to learn and grow. There are many teachers throughout the world who are in line with this idea.

When I researched who I wished to study with I looked for: Reiki Practice offerings, continuing education, and activity in the community. This is your opportunity to explore this incredible energy, choosing the right teacher will make a huge difference on how to move forward and what direction you go with it.

Transitioning to Eve.

What Susanne wrote is a beautiful way to explore energy work. I also took time to find the teachers that offered continuing education. Taking Reiki Levels 1-3 multiple times from different teachers rounded out my knowledge base and helped me see there are many approaches that offer results.

What makes this energy so incredible — I know I've mentioned this before — is that Reiki, the energy itself teaches you how to use it. Learning has been a magical process that I am still in awe about. I cannot image, looking forward, what else may be possible.

That being said, having a mentor to bounce ideas off of really helped me expand my practice! We would love to hear from you if you have any questions, comments, or concerns.

Speaking on behalf of all the practitioners who have contributed to this book: We wish you safe and loving passage on whatever path you find yourself!

Chapter 22

References & Further Reading

These are the references quoted directly in this book. They represent only a small portion of the references used throughout my twenty years of study. I hold great love and gratitude for each teacher and how they have nurtured my learning. For this, and because it is important to honor those we learn from, I include many of the books and places that have taught or inspired me so that you can explore them for yourself.

Hunt, V. R. (1996). Infinite Mind: Science of the Human Vibrations of Consciousness. Malibu Publishing.

Jain, S. (2021). Healing Ourselves: Biofield Science and the Future of Health. Sounds True, Boulder.

Li Q. (2010). Effect of forest bathing trips on human immune function. *Environmental health and preventive medicine*, *15*(1), 9–17. https://doi.org/10.1007/s12199-008-0068-3.

Lübeck, W., Petter, F. A., Rand, W. L. (2001). The spirit of Reiki: The complete handbook of the Reiki system. Pilgrims Publishing, Kathmandu.

Nestor, J. (2021). Breath: The new science of a lost art. Penguin Random House, Dublin.

Ober, C., Sinatra, S. T., & Zucker, M. (2010). Earthing: The Most Important Health Discovery Ever!. Basic Health Publications, United States.

Petter, F. A. (1997). Reiki fire: New information about the origins of the Reiki power a complete manual. Lotus Press, Shangri-La.

Pert, C. (2003). Molecules of emotion: The science behind mind-body medicine. Scribner, New York.

Three Initiates. (2018). The Kybalion Hermetic Philosophy. Centenary Edition. A TarcherPerigee Book, New York.

Unknown. (2012). The Yoga Sutras of Patanjali. Commentary by Satchidananda. Integral Yoga Publications. United States.

Zajonc, A. (March 17, 2011). Thinking like Einstein. Psychology Today Online. Accessed November 2, 2024. https://www.psychologytoday.com/us/blog/the-meditative-life/201103/thinking-einstein#:~:text=We%20think%20of%20meditation%20as,expanded%20equally%20on%20all%20sides

Other Impactful References

Film

Heal (2017) Directed by Noonan-Gores

The Wisdom of Trauma (2021) Directed by Zaya & Maurizio Benazzo

My Octopus Teacher (2020) Directed by Pippa Ehrlich & James Reed

Surviving Death (2021) Directed by Ricki Stern

Written

Awareness: The Perils and Opportunities of Reality (1990) by Anthony de Mello

Braiding Sweetgrass: Indigenous Wisdom, Scientific Knowledge, and the Teachings of Plants (2013) by Robin Wall Kimmerer

Burnout, Burnout, Burnout: The Secret to Unlocking the Stress Cycle (2020) by Emily Nagoski, PhD & Amelia Nagoski, DMA

Dying to Be Me: My Journey from Cancer, To Near Death, To True Healing (2012) by Anita Moorjani

Decolonizing Wellness: A QTBIPOC-Centered Guide to Escape the Diet Trap, Heal Your Self-Image, and Achieve Body Liberation (2022) by Dalia Kinsey, RD., LD

Sacred Medicine: A Doctor's Quest to Unravel the Mysteries of Healing (2022) by Lissa Rankin, MD

Slow Medicine: The Way to Healing (2017) by Victoria Sweet, MD

The Biology of Belief (2005) 2015 ed. by Bruce H Lipton, PhD

Cure: A Journey into the Science of Mind over Body (2016) by Jo Marchant

The Body Keeps The Score: Mind, Brain and Body in the Transformation of Trauma (2014) by Bessel Van Der Kolk

The Yoga Sutras of Patanjali (2020) by Satchidananda

The Road Home (2015) by Ethan Nichtern

The Four Agreements (1997) by Don Miguel Ruiz

Molecules of Emotion: The Science Behind Mind-body Medicine (2003) by Candace B Pert, PhD

Gut: The Inside Story of Our Body's Most Under-rated Organ (2015) by Giulia Enders

The Science of Meditation: How to Change Your Brain, Mind and Body (2017) by Daniel Golemand, PhD & Richard J. Davidson, PhD

The Energy Cure: Unraveling the Mystery of Hands-On Healing (2010) by William Bengston, PhD

The Untethered Soul: The Journey Beyond Yourself (2007) by Michael A Singer

The Surrender Experiment (2015) by Michael A Singer

Being Peace by Thich Nhat Hanh

No Mud, No Lotus by Thich Nhat Hanh

A Meditator's Guide (2013) Compiled and translated by Jess Peter Koffman

When the Body Says No: The Cost of Hidden Stress (2019) by Gabor Maté

Books Written in Takata's Lineage

The Reiki Manual: A Training Guide for Reiki Students, Practitioners, and Masters (2003) by Penelope Quest and Kathy Roberts

Reiki: The Legacy of Hawayo Takata (2004) by Christine L. O'Sullivan and other practitioners.

Chapter 23

What's Next?

Becoming Involved with Reiki and Other
Energy Practices

Learn Reiki with Eve at my Atlanta, Georgia studio. Connect
with me at www.sanctumwithevesmyth.com for Reiki classes or private sessions.

Other Energetic Studies Online

The Language of the Mind-Body: Unlocking Clear Commu-
nication through Sound

My sound study group offers you a path to understanding the
unique language of your body, higher self, and subconscious mind, so
you can live with less stress and stand confidently in your power.

Have you ever had an experience in a meditation with sound where
you saw colors, lights, or images? Have you felt the body release? These
are normal occurrences as you work with sound meditations and are
a type of communication from the subconscious mind. Because you
may not know what a color or image may mean, a communication
with the body or higher self may not occur. Through this transformative study group, you will receive curated sound meditations intended

for you to learn how to listen and receive tools to interpret the subtle messages your body and subconscious are sending you.

Using sound as a tool, you'll explore how your body communicates through symbols, feelings, colors, movements, sensations, and even metaphorical images. By understanding this inner language, you'll not only reduce stress but also see where there may be room for become more attuned to your life's true purpose.

You can find the course on Teachable at my school, Sanctum with Eve

Substack: A Journey of Sound, Stories, and Spirit

Sanctum with Eve is a space for exploring and deepening your intuition. Whether you're just beginning or continuing your journey, this newsletter supports your development of intuition, recognition of flow, and release of fear around the unknown.

Sanctum represents a sacred space within, where clarity and guidance are available, even amidst life's chaos. Through shared stories, sound, and spiritual practices, I aim to create peace, harmony, and balance in the body and mind.

Receive insight 2-3 Sundays a month, including collective energy readings, real-life lessons from Spirit, sound healing, and symbolic language development.

Drawing from my own experiences, I'll guide you in accessing your inner sanctum, nurturing your connection to the higher self, and approaching the unknown with curiosity.

https://open.substack.com/pub/evesmyth